ECONOMICS OF CULTURE INDUSTRY

Economics of Culture Industry

Television in India

K.V. Joseph

SHIPRA

ISBN: 978-81-7541-565-2

First Published in India in 2010

Economics of Culture Industry: Television in India

Published by:
SHIPRA PUBLICATIONS
H.O.: LG 18-19, Pankaj Central Market, Patparganj,
I.P. Ext., Delhi-110092, Tel: 91-11-2223 5152, 2223 6152
Br.Off.: 4617/18, Ansari Road, Darya Ganj,
New Delhi-110002, Tel: 6594 6453, 9810522367
E-mail: info@shiprapublications.com
www.shiprapublications.com

Foreword

Television is one of the epoch-making inventions of the twentieth century. It has permeated every corner of public and private space within a short period of its invention. With further advancements in technology, it has grown as a international phenomenon rendering national boundaries somewhat irrelevant. In a sense, the world has been transformed into a globalised village for which the credit should go squarely to television than any other determinant. A far more important aspect relates to the emergence of television as a major economic activity in many parts of the world.

The main thrust of the book is to uncover the parameters in transforming television as an economic function. The author contends that there is a fusion of art, technology and economics in its emergence as an economic activity. Art and culture are supposed to rely mainly on mental faculties rather than on material resources. However, technological advancements have paved the way for giving culture and arts an economic dimension as well. Moreover, economic norms may have acquired the upper hand as determinants in shaping and guiding the production of cultural commodities. In television, an important branch of culture industry, economic norms and cultural genres which normally operate under different premises coalesce with each other. Apparently, as the author maintains norms and yardsticks differing from regular industries would be required to understand the functioning of television.

As an industry, television specializes in the production of a wide variety of cultural products with creative contents and symbolic meanings. They are known as texts in the technical language of the industry. What television does is to telecast them as programmes 24 hours of the day. Motivated by the desire to secure maximum gains, entertainment in some form or other is invariably incorporated as the main ingredient of most of the programmes. Apparently artistic norms get diluted at the behest of market considerations.

Being an activity guided by commercial considerations, marketing becomes crucial in television also. Marketing in television is not so simple as the product itself is a service which can render value only when it is actually utilized by the audience. At the same time, most of the channels offer their programmes as a free good which the consumers can utilize whenever they like. What the channels usually do is to resort to a kind of dual product marketing by which they offer their products to the consumers as a free good on the one hand and to sell their telecast time or airtime to the advertisers for a high price on the other. Thus advertisers become the de facto purchasers in the market who sustain the industry by recouping practically the entire cost. The author has made a detailed analysis of the marketing mechanism of the industry with an array of facts and figures from various sources.

Being a branch of culture industry, artists provide the kernel of labour input though other forms of labour enter in the picture too. Apparently, the peculiarities of the art labour market and the system of payment of remuneration to artists are another set of issues which a study of television has to uncover. The issue becomes complicated because wide variations in the payment of remuneration to different categories of artists are inherent in the industry.

How the audience looks upon television and its impact on various facets of life are delineated with the findings of a field study. TV is a powerful medium capable of making far reaching changes in the life of man. Some of them may be harmful to the society at large. A far more serious aspect relates to the adverse impact of television on young children who are very often exposed to programmes with themes of crime, violence and immorality. The problem is how to protect children from such television coverage. Should the state as the guardian of the community leave everything to the free play of the market? The problem becomes complicated because artistic freedom of expression has to be reconciled with the demands of the market. The author is in favour of regulations on the industry as most the programmes are merely commercial commodities meant for sale in the market rather than original works of art.

Television reached India in a humble way in 1959 under a UNESCO aided experimental programme. Growth of the industry has been very slow during the initial stages. It began to expand beyond recognition with the liberalization initiated during 1990s. Since then it has grown as a gigantic industry with, according to the author, a capital investment of more than Rs. 380,000 million. According to his findings people sit in front of the magic box on an average of 1hour 48 minutes a day. On an average a person spends Rs. 100 in a year for seeing TV programmes. These of course are far below the American standards.

The author has made an earnest attempt to delineate the different aspects of television as a branch of the culture industry and to uncover various issues involved in the working of television by drawing evidence from the Indian experience. He has also made a systematic study of the growth of television in India. The book is perhaps the first of its kind dealing with the economics of television as a branch of culture industry. It is sure to get a good response not only from the scholarly community but also from the general public. Credit should go to the author for making such a serious study and presenting it in a simple style.

Vinod Thomas
Director-General and Senior Vice-President
World Bank

Preface

Ever since its invention on the eve of the of the Second World War, television has grown as a gigantic enterprise in almost all parts of the world. Its penetration is limited not only to the metropolitan cities of the developed world but also to the remote villages of the Third World. It provides a wide variety of menu comprising news, discussions, artistic performances, tele-serials, motion pictures, and instructional materials etc. suitable to meet the tastes and needs of different categories of people. The attraction of television stems from its capacity to deliver the product in any part of the world simultaneously in live form. In turn, all categories of people spend regularly a few hours a day in front of the TV.

Being an activity impinging on different activities like culture, art, communication, politics, economics and so on, scholars belonging to different disciplines have attempted to uncover the meaning and implications of television from their own disciplinary angles. However, the economic aspect seems to be far more important for various reasons. Television calls for investment of huge amounts of money for the establishment of broadcasting stations, preparation of the texts and their transmission or conveyance. It provides employment to hundreds of thousands of people for the gathering, preparation, processing and transmission of texts. When huge sums of money are thus invested and hundreds of thousands of people are employed, television is sure to generate output and income on a substantial scale. Ipso facto, the whole exercise becomes an economic activity par excellence.

However, the programmes and their contents are not goods in the material sense. They are in the nature of services, which have to be utilized as and when they are transmitted. At the same time, they are products of creative works relying more on intellectual means for their creation and they carry symbolic meanings. Such products fall within the realm of culture.

Thus television resembles a Janus-faced activity, relying on material means for the creation of cultural products. Activities meant for the production of culture and art for sale in the market form what is termed culture industry in which cultural genres and economic norms coalesce. Television is one of such activities which falls within the contours of culture industry. The process of production, the modus operandi of marketing, determination of output, pricing of the product in television, etc. would naturally be differing from those of any ordinary industry. How economic parameters and cultural genres, each encompassing different orientations coalesce with each other forms the theme of the present study.

Television reached India in 1959 in a humble way under a UNESCO aided scheme. It was a state monopoly till 1990 displaying very little progress. With the liberalization of 1990s, private channels also began to enter in the field and since then the progress was phenomenal. The conditions under which television grew and developed in India were altogether different from those of its development in the West. The study therefore aims at uncovering the modus operandi of culture industry from that of the Indian experience.

The author of the study is indebted to various organizations and individuals for pursuing the study. Among them, the Indian Council of Social Science Research, New Delhi stands foremost. The study was taken up under a research project with financial support from the ICSSR. The author takes this opportunity to record his deep sense of gratitude and indebtedness to the ICSSR without whose financial support the study would not have been completed. The author is grateful to Dr. Sara John, former Deputy Director, Dr. Jessy George, Deputy Director and Sri. P.M. Ramteke and Dr. P.J. Meshram former Assistant Directors of the ICSSR for having been very helpful at different stages during the tenureship of the project.

The project was affiliated to the Centre for Development Studies Trivandrum. The author expresses his deep sense of gratitude to the authorities of the Centre for Development Studies and in particular to Dr. K.P. Kannan, former Director, Dr. K.N. Narayanan Nair, the current Director and Sri Soman Nair, Registrar of the CDS for all the help rendered to him for pursuing the study to the final stage.

Thanks are due to a large number of persons who were very helpful for providing information on various aspects of the working of television. They include Sri Rameswar Rao, Additional Director General and Ms Shalinini Narayanan, Director, Directorate of Advertising and Visual Publicity, Ministry of Information and Broadcasting, New Delhi, Sri Thomas John, and Sri Jyothis Kumar of DoordarshanKendra, Trivandrum, Sri Baby Mathew, Managing Director, Jeevan TV, Sri. P. Mohanan of Asianet. Sri Sebastian Thennassery of Amrita TV, Prof. Karunan Thampi, Dr. C.S. Venkiteswaran, Sri. K. Kunhikrishnan, and so on.

A study of such a nature cannot be pursueded without utilizing the materials available in various libraries. In this connection, the author expresses his deep sense of obligation to the devoted members of the staff of the CDS library and in particular to Sri Anil Kumar and Sri Gopa Kumar. Thanks are also due to the staff of the administration and accounts sections of the CDS.

The author is also thankful to Dr. Varghese Mathunny, the Research Officer of the project who has been a very good source of help at different stages, particularly in the preparation and drafting of Chapter 8, "Audience Response to Television Programmes: An Empirical Analysis".

Dr. K.V. Joseph

Centre for Development Studies,
Trivandrum

Contents

List of Tables

1

Introduction

Non-material activities like those related to art, literature, ritual performance, dramatic enactment, learning process etc., which rely mainly on mental faculties fall within the realm of culture. Free labour as opposed to craft labour or mercenary labour engages in such activities. With the growth of technology, material means are being utilized on an increasing scale in the creation or production of such cultural activities. Furthermore, altogether new products which though cultural in origin rely on material means, like photographs, motion pictures, telefilms, etc., have come into existence. Even artistic performances like music or dance can be converted into material form with the help of technological devices. Such cultural products are being produced as regular commodities on factory lines and sold in the market for profit. In so doing, the creation of culture becomes some sort of an economic activity. "The economic process by which cultural goods and services are made, marketed, distributed and sold to the consumers", as Throsby puts it, falls within the ambit of what is known as culture industry.[1] In other words, the term culture industry stands for, as Steinert enjoins "the subsumption of diverse kinds of intellectual production under commodity principles".[2]

A number of activities engaging in the production of culture as commodities have emerged with the technological progress. Television which informs, educates and entertains people is recognized as one among the different kinds of activities forming within the broad contour of culture industry. Television per se, is a technological instrument through which cultural products like films, telefilms, serials and various cultural progrmmes can be transmitted to audiences situated in far away places and who can see them by operating another instrument, the TV set. Television, as it is usually referred to, comprises the instrument along with the cultural content. Cultural genres and economic norms coalesce with one another in the creation of the cultural programmes transmitted through television. In doing so, as Barker enjoins "culture is bound up with economic production".[3] How these two distinct functions which operate under altogether different premises coalesce with one another and the manner in which such activities are being carried on, are questions of topical importance having far reaching implications.

Television which originated during the middle of twentieth century has grown as a gigantic enterprise in many parts of the world. Huge investments are being made in television networks and cable TVs whose turnover runs into billion dollars. Furthermore, millions of people engage themselves in the making, processing and transmission of TV programmes. At the same time, people all over the world tend to curtail many of their less urgent engagements to find time for viewing television programmes. It is reported for instance, that people in the U.S. A used to spend on an average nearly seven hours a day for viewing television programmes during the heyday of television.[4] Even newspaper circulation is said to have declined in the wake of TV boom. In fact, television 'colonises' leisure time.[5] Developments of similar nature would have taken place in India which has emerged as the country with fourth largest number of television sets. Though television came to India only in 1959 under an educational programme of UNESCO, it has grown into gigantic proportions with structural changes far beyond recognition. Not less than 200 channels or companies compete with one another in transmitting programmes daily in different languages. All of them are organized as big business concerns with the shares of some of them even listed in the stock market.

Theme of the Study

Ipsofacto, the present study was undertaken to uncover the

theme, "Economics of Culture Industry: A Study with Reference to Television in India". The feasibility of connecting culture with industry can create doubts in the minds of many. Similarly, the word culture itself lacks precision. Apparently, the theme of the study is impregnant with many complex problems.

Being one among the different branches of culture industry, the organisational structure and modus operandi of television channels would be different from that of any other industrial unit or firm. Furthermore, television is a product of advanced technology. Technological involvement calls for high cost of production at various stages. No enterprise can be carried on without recouping the cost of production. Marketing is the usual mechanism used for this purpose. However, the problem with TV is, how the product is to be marketed effectively, as a programme in a channel can be seen in any part of the world with the help of a television set. Apparently, how the cost is to be recouped, let alone the product is to be marketed for a profit becomes another problem to be encountered.

The products themselves are intangible commodities with no physical output in the strict sense, unlike in the case of manufacturing industry. They are mere service products whose output depends on the actual utilisation. Apparently, measurement of output, let alone valuation of output remains totally elusive. Some sort of ad hoc measures like the time spent for viewing the programmes appear to be the only way out under such circumstances.

At the same time, the products are supposed to be cultural in origin. Cultural products are unique in nature On the other hand, standardisation is the norm usually adopted in the case of usual commodities. Naturally, how to reconcile the demands of the market on the one hand, and the requirements of artistic creation on the other forms another problem confronting television industry.

Remuneration to labour input is awarded on the basis of productivity. In television, programmes are turned out as the joint output of art labour and ordinary labour. What should be the criterion for rewarding different categories of labour inputs utilised in the creation of television programmes is another problem faced by the industry.

Findings of Earlier Studies

Studies on television are galore. Most of them deal with the cultural aspects of television (Mullan 1996, Barker 1997, Bignell 2004, Mitra Anand 1993 etc.). Some of them focus on the technological or communication aspects of television. (Lodziak Conrad 1986, Raymond Williams; 1975). Television is looked upon as a diffusing agent and thereby a development fostering agency by some other authors. (Melkote Srinivas, 1991; Sinhai, Aravind 1981). Studies focusing on the economic aspects like making, gathering, processing and transmitting the programmes and thereby in creating employment and generating income by television are scanty.

Nevertheless, authors like Horkheimer Max and T.W. Adorno of the Frankfurt school could sense the emergence of an industry around entertainment activities, which they termed "Culture Industry". In their opinion, the culture industry is dedicated to "elevated pleasure". In doing so, the culture industry downgrades art to the level of a mercantile commodity. In their words, "what is new is not that it is a commodity, but that today it deliberately admits it is one, that art renounces its own autonomy and proudly takes its place among consumption goods...".[6] Notwithstanding the negative connotations, the authors highlight the significance of cultural products as distinct from ordinary material goods. They wrote on culture industry when television was in its infant stage and apparently they were unable to comprehend its future developments. However, the whole exercise seems to ignore the importance of economic aspects of the culture industry. Authors like Steinert, Hesmondhalgh, etc., have made improvements on the theme introduced by Horkheimer and Adorno. Hesmondhalgh regards the plural term cultural industries instead of the singular term culture industry as a better term for conveying the full implication of culture industry.[7] However, he was concerned with culture industry as a whole and not with television. Though Steinert has sensed the role of television in transforming the nature of art and entertainment as a whole, and of converting politics as a kind of entertainment, he has not attempted to elucidate the implication of television as a sub sector of culture industry.[8]

Taking a slightly different stand, Alvin Gouldner, makes a subtle distinction between cultural apparatus and consciousness industry. Cultural apparatus comprising educational institutions, newspapers, etc., form the actual manufacturers of knowledge. On the other hand, the consciousness industry produces mass art like cinema, television etc.[9] The author, while acknowledging the economic implication of consciousness industry, fails to appreciate the involvement of cultural elements in such an industry.

Moving further ahead, Throsby who gave a better definition to culture industry states that, "the term cultural industry in contemporary usage does indeed carry with it a sense of economic potential of cultural production to generate output, employment and revenue and to satisfy the demands of consumers, whatever other nobler purpose may be served by the activities of the artists and by the exercise of the tastes of the connoisseurs".[10] Inspite of the clarification offered by him, his explanations by itself is insufficient to uncover the problems raised earlier. Nor, has he given any attention to TV.

Concepts and Issues

Though none the authors have attempted to uncover the problems, some of their formulations can be helpful for pursuing the study. Being a study focusing on culture industry with special reference to television, the main thrust would be on the lines conceptualized by the authors of the Frankfurt school. However, the need to rely on the concepts formulated by other scholars becomes inevitable for proceeding further as Horkheimer and Adorno have not elaborated their concepts. The base-superstructure dichotomy constitutes one of the important theoretical formulations suitable to a study on culture industry. Cultural activities which fall within the realm of super-structure do not engage in material production. Though the artists have to rely on material means produced by ordinary labour for their subsistence, cultural activities operate as autonomous activities. However, the application of advanced technological instruments in the creation, or rather the production of cultural activities resulting in the commodification of art has rendered the autonomy somewhat weak.[11] Entertainment rather than cathartic purpose has become the main motive behind the cultural products turned out under the new dispensation. Cultural genres get somewhat marginalized in such cases. Nevertheless, the dichotomy can serve as a starting point for pursuing the study.

What television does, amounts to a service activity oriented towards culture. In this context, the formulation of what Anna Burger calls "Janus faced" cultural service, seems to be relevant for exploring the activities of television. In her opinion, "material ways of conveyance and the intellectual contents to be conveyed are of equal importance" in such cultural services.[12] Being a service product, the output of the industry comprising contents conveyed renders any value as and when they are actually utilized by the audience. Since material means are utilized on a significant scale, the need for raising capital as well as recouping at least the cost element becomes imperative in a culture industry like television.

However, the term "services" connotes flow rather than the stock of a commodity. The programmes which television broadcasts are only flows from a recorded stock termed "text" which can "give rise over time to a flow of services". Apparently, what Throsby calls "cultural capital" which "embodies stores or provides cultural value in addition to whatever economic value it may possess" would be an appropriate concept for analyzing the economic and cultural aspects associated with television.[13]

As a technological instrument, television provides the means for communicating at multiple points. Communication, so to say, is a function of culture pertaining to art. Since the function of television is to communicate at multiple points to an audience located in distant places, it becomes an important unit of what is known as mass media. With television, art reaches the audience in a mediated form. Conceptual formulations relating to mass media, therefore also become relevant in understanding the functions of television. However, play element rather than work element of communication takes the upper hand in television programmes as the needs of large number of people are being catered.[14]

Since a medium like television can reach millions of people, businessmen make use of the service of TV for the purpose of advertisement on an increasing scale. Advertisement has therefore emerged as an important source of income to television. Ipsofacto, advertisement has become a crucial element in understanding the financial aspects relating to television. In the light of the aforesaid discussion, the study revolves around a number of issues, the important among them are the following: How an industry could grow around television and what is its organizational structure? What is the modus operandi of television as an industrial activity? How can the value of the output be measured? What role do the material means and cultural services play in the working of television? How far can television texts be regarded as cultural capital distinct from real capital? How do the financial requirements of television channels are met and which methods are adopted for recouping the cost element? What role does advertisement play in securing the financial resources needed for television?

What is the economic significance of television in the country in terms of income and employment? What is the impact of television on society and culture at large in the era of globalisation? Should there be any regulation or control over production and transmission of television programmes?

Methodology

Since the issues call for answers encompassing economic and cultural aspects, investigation relying on a single disciplinary angle may not serve the purpose. Instead, the desirability of "a multi-dimensional and multi-perspectival approach to the understanding of television" as advocated by Barker serves as a meaningful alternative.[15] Accordingly, divergent methods and approaches with suitable modifications became the basis of investigation of the study both at macro and micro levels.

At the macro level, the approach was to examine how an industry could grow around television by tracing the various stages of its evolution. An appropriate comparison of the growth of television in other countries has also been made in all feasible cases. It could shed further insights on the growth of television as an industry.

Survey method was adopted at the micro level to uncover various aspects relating to the audience response to television. Purposive random sample survey with structured schedules was made for his purpose. Different categories of audience formed the universe for the study. Audience was divided on the basis of age, sex, educational qualification, occupational distribution. Timing of various programmes and contents of different programmes formed the other criteria for dividing the audience into different categories. Questionnaires suitable to collect details like their preferences for different programmes, the time devoted to see the programmes etc. were prepared. In addition a few directors, financiers, artists, and television critics were interviewed.

Secondary sources provided much of the data required for the study. Data available in the records of some television channels formed an important source. Audience Research Survey of Doordarshan and various reports of the Ministry of Information and Broadcasting formed another important source. Details available in various reports and studies could be collected as another source of data. Besides newspaper reports were also helpful in providing information on various aspects of the industry. Secondary sources were supplemented with the primary source comprising those collected through surveys and interviews with structured schedules.

Scheme of the Study

The study contains ten chapters in all. The theme of the study, the problems pertaining to the theme, the concepts applicable to the study, the main issues to be investigated and the methodology are delineated in the Introduction. Chapter 2 gives a brief outline of the approaches to culture industry. Culture and art in their various manifestations serve as a tranquilising agent in man's life. Culture had a humble origin and evolved over the years from the wall-paintings of the paleolithic period to the commodification of modern period. Culture industry in which culture sustained by technology coalescing with economic yardsticks constitutes the latest stage in the evolution of culture. What are the salient features of culture industry and how television fits in as a branch of culture industry are the other aspects covered in the Chapter. How television could grow on industrial lines and what are the salient features of television as an industrial activity form the theme of Chapter 3. As indicated in the Chapter television has grown as an industry from the fusion of art, technology and economics. Scientific experimentations relating to television were in the offing from the closing decades of nineteenth century. They culminated with the public broadcasting of TV in 1936. Though the Second World War halted the progress temporarily, television could grow in rapid strides after the end of hostilities. Television could acquire new dimensions with the introduction of cable and satellite telecasting. Sensing the economic prospects of TV, the American business concerns and entrepreneurial classes were in the forefront in organizing it on industrial lines. The Chapter also gives an account of the introduction of different programmes. Chapter 4 provides a brief account of the growth and development of television in India. Economic significance of television in terms capital investment, output and employment are also delineated in the chapter. How economic parameters and cultural genres coalesce forms the most important side of the study. The divergent premises of these two disciplines are supposed to operate jointly in the production and marketing of television texts. While Chapter 5 delineates the production side, Chapter 6 focuses on the marketing side respectively. Television is engaged in the production of different kinds of texts. They are broadcast as programmes throughout the day. The different forms of programmes and the manner in which they are produced and telecast are also explained in detail in Chapter 5. Being an activity guided also by business considerations marketing is crucial in the case of television. Marketing in television is not so simple as the product is a flow of services. Advertiser also enters into the fray as a key player in a different role—as a purchaser of telecast time. These complex nature of the marketing side of television is also delineated in detail in the Chapter. The peculiarities of art market and the system of paying remuneration to artists form the theme of Chapter 7. How the audiences, the consumers look upon television and its impact on various facets of life were uncovered in Chapter 8. The contents of the chapter comprise mostly the findings of a field survey. In it an account of the socio-economic profile of the audience, their attitude towards different kinds of programmes, their viewing habits etc. are delineated. Television makes far reaching impact on the social, cultural, economic, and political life of man. With the ongoing process of liberalization and globalsation, state has withdrawn from the commanding position as the informer, educator, and entertainer through television. At the same time, with the development of satellite technology, programmes from any part of the world can penetrate in other parts easily. National frontiers have thus become irrelevant in controlling the entry of programmes from outside. Furthermore, TV channels transmit immoral themes and project sex and violence with impunity. Young children who see such programmes become the victims of such programmes. Under such circumstances the question, should the state leave everything to the free play of the market poses as a major issue. Similarly, another question, does not the state have a moral obligation to safeguard the well-being of the citizens by regulating and even controlling TV also surfaces. In Chapter 9, answers to these questions and other issues are sought. A brief summary and main conclusions are detailed in the concluding Chapter.

Significance of the Study

The study is of topical importance for a variety of reasons. Cultural economics is a newly emerging sub-discipline of economics. According to Boulding it is still in the embryonic stage.[16] However, the emergence of culture industry which deals with a variety of cultural products, is a new development which may be viewed as the beginning of a new sub-discipline. The manner in which cultural genres and economic norms are fused in the creation and marketing of cultural products is the main theme of the present study. The uncovering of such developments, can be helpful for an understanding of the beginnings of the new sub-discipline of economics.

The study could bring to lime light the significance of television as an economic activity. To some extent, it could shed light on the socio-cultural impact of television including those relating to various aspects of socio-cultural life. With the growth of television, self-sustaining privatism has emerged as a new form of behavioural pattern. Many people, as mentioned earlier, curtail their social activities, for finding time to view television programmes. According to some observers, "structured wants" have taken deep roots in those societies where television has made inroads.[17] The study, appears to be helpful to enlighten us on such changes in social, economic and cultural life wrought about by the media revolution.

The role of advertisement in the whole process is another issue of major significance. Advertisement has emerged as a major input and at the same time a source for securing financial resources for TV channels. Life style also is being reshaped beyond recognition as a result of the inflow of advertisements. The study also sheds light on the emerging role of advertisement resulting from the rise of television as an important channel of communication.

By and large, the emergence of television channels as major economic enterprises ensued only with the liberalization of the economy. At the same time, television itself can be used as an agency for promoting the ongoing process of liberalization and globalisation. However, the limits to which globalization should or could be pursued is a controversial issue. It is believed that the proposed study could throw some light on these questions also.

Notwithstanding the spectacular growth of television as a major component of the culture industry, the full implications of culture industry still remain by and large as an unresearched area. The study, a pioneering exploration in this field, could it is hoped to widen the area of knowledge in the matter.

NOTES AND REFERENCES

1. David, Throsby (2001). *Economics and Culture,* Cambridge, University Press, p. 111.
2. Heinz, Steinert (2003). *Culture Industry,* Cambridge, Polity Press, p. 10.
3. Barker, Chris (1997). *Global Television: An Introduction,* Oxford, Blackwell Publishers, p. 5.
4. Roy, Wilson and Stein, L.E. (1989). *Mass Media and Mass Cultııre,* New York, Random House, p. 217.
5. Conrad, Lodziak (1986). *The Power of Television: A Critical Appraisal,* London Frances Pinter, p. 130.
6. Adorno, T.W. and Horkheimer Max (1977). "The Culture Industry: Enlightenment As Mass Deception" in James Curran (ed.) *Mass Communication and Society,* London, Open University, p. 376.
7. David, Hesmondhalgh (2002). *The Cultural Industries,* London, Sage Publications, pp. 15-16.
8. Heinz, Steinert (2003). *Op. cit.,* p. 32.
9. Alvin, Gouldner (1990). "Ideology, Cultural Apparatus and New Consciousness Industry" in Jeffrey Alexander (ed). *Culture and Society,* Cambridge University Press, pp. 306-316.
10. David, Throsby (2001). *op. cit.,* p. 10.
11. Joseph, K.V. (1990). "Economics of Art" in P.R. Gopinathan Nair (ed.), *Economy, Planning and Policies,* Delhi, Concept, pp. 127-35.
12. Burger, Anna (1970). *Economic Problems of Consumer Services,* Budapest, Akademai Kiado, p. 41.
13. David, Throsby (2001). *op. cit.,* p. 46.
14. Schramm Wilbur quotes from Stephnson. W. "Theory of Communication", Chicago, University, Press, in *Men, Women, Messages and Media: Understanding Human Communication* (1982), New York, Harper Press, p. 24.
15. Chris, Barker (1997). *op. cit.,* p. 6.

16. Boulding, Kenneth (1973). "Towards the Development of a Cultural Economics" in Louis Sneider (ed.), *Idea of Culture in Social Sciences*, Cambridge University Press, p. 55.
17. Claus, Offe (1984). *Contradictions of Welfare State*, London, Huchison, quoted by Lodziak Conrad in *Power of Television*, *op. cit.*, p. 172.

2

From Culture to Culture Industry

In previous chapter, the theme of the study along with the main issues and the methodology was delineated. What is meant by culture, its relation to economics, and the evolution of culture industry, its implication and the complexion of the industry are explored in this chapter.

What is Meant by Culture

To begin with, the term culture industry stands for the production of culture on industrial lines for commercial gains. However, the word culture is not very precise and lacks a clear cut demarcation. In the opinion of an author "the attempts to define culture are akin to trying to encage the wind".[1] Since the borderline is not clear, the term culture is used in different senses. Originally the term culture was used to indicate the tillage of the soil, meaning agriculture. From that of the cultivation of land, it was thought of as an expression of the cultivation of the mind and intellect. Subsequently, the term came to be used in different senses. Among the different senses in which the term is now used, the anthropological line of definition is perhaps the most important one. In the words of an authority, culture stands for "the learned repertories of thought and action exhibited by the members of social groups transmitted from generation to generation".[2] Apparently, norms, behavioural patterns, values, beliefs, knowledge etc., exhibited by a group of people fall within the ambit of culture. They are so to say the way of life of a group of people comprising all forms of improvements on nature made by man. Group in turn can be identified in terms of the differences in language, religion, nationality etc. Culture denoting in terms of beliefs and norms of behaviour cannot in the normal course be produced as a commodity.

Another important sense in which the term culture is used relates it to certain activities. It is used in the objective form. Activities of creative nature which carry some symbolic meaning and in many cases contain intellectual properties fall within the ambit of culture according to the second sense. Such activities result in the creation of goods and services. Production under assembly line is feasible in the case of such activities as a result of technological advancements. Culture under this sense encompasses literature, painting, music, acting, dancing and all other kinds of art. They satisfy the human need for expression, affirmation and communication.[3] In a sense, culture of such a nature is synonymous with art. Art on its part, creates some sort of equilibrium in the life of man. In the words of an author, "in the systematized spaces and volume of a painting, in the clarified procession of sounds in the music, in the condenced joy of poetry, we have order, we have harmony and peace".[4] As a matter of fact, ordinary life is full of worries and tensions. Art can restore some amount of solace and tranquility in real life. Joyce Carey succinctly elaborates: "art has immense power for good and evil because it always deals with fundamental passions and reactions common to all humanity. In its more complex forms, it carries man permanently out of the squalor and boredom of material needs and appetites out of a mechanical existence where he becomes by imagination a hero or saint".[5] In other words, works of art can make life sober and balanced.

Fischer approaches the problem from the angle of man's thirst for becoming a full man. He is not satisfied merely by remaining as a separate individual. From that of satisfying with the partial life of an individual existence, man strives towards fullness which can be attained only if he takes possession of the experience of others that might be potentially his own. This can be achieved by merging with the world around him. In turn, art as Fischer puts, "is the indispensable means, for this merging of the individual with the whole".[6]

Evolution of Culture as a Commodity

Art as such is not concerned with material production. At the same time, there should be an economic base to support the growth of artistic activities as artists do not engage in the production of material goods. In other words, artists themselves have to be supported by the material goods produced by the ordinary labour. Apparently, a rise in the level of productivity is of crucial importance for the development of art. As Hawkes and Woolley concur "while material prosperity can never be the cause of artistic genius, society cannot support its artists without an economic margin". They go further and add" there is no doubt that the abundance of game to be hunted in south west Europe in late Pleistocene times, made a necessary foundation for the development of Paleolithic art".[7] Marx also expresses the same and states thus; "it is however less to the size of its population, than to the possibility of employing a relatively large proportion of it in unproductive work that ancient Egypt owes its great works of architecture".[8] Apparently, some sort of division of labour as to how the product is to be shared between the artists and other members of the society becomes inevitable. Art was primarily social in function from its very inception. In ancient Greece for example, as Osbourne puts it "drama was performed under the state auspices at national religious festivals which were attended by the whole citizen body". Similarly, "poetry was not made to be read at home by the few who happen to like it. Poetry was sung at all social gatherings public and private and at all religious ceremonies".[9] Since art was a social activity there was no difficulty in sharing the produce in the society. However, in course of time the old order broke up and patronage of art was taken up by the rulers, the religious authorities, the nobles and so on. When capitalism became dominant, market forces became the arbiter in determining the share of the artists. Other changes were also at work in modifying the relationship of art with the material base. With market replacing the patron in supporting artistic and cultural activities, the evolution of cultural activities as an industrial activity was only a question of time. At the same time, certain inventions have played key roles in the diversification of artistic activities. Though artists need only simple means like a pen for their creative activities they also rely on technology for pursuing their occupations. In turn the, new technological inventions have been of immense help for the improvement and even growth of art. Invention of the printing press is perhaps the most important among them. With this copies of the original could be made easily. Books of all kinds including artistic works could be printed. Needless to say, any invention can lead to various developments which the original inventors do not anticipate. What followed with the invention of printing press was the emergence of publishing business and the eventual growth of newspaper industry. With this, market could replace the patron in sustaining the creative writers. When market gained strength, commercial institutions of various categories sprang up. In turn, as Eisenstein puts, "the literary artist whether poet, fiction writer or historical romancer not only exploited the new media most fully and deliberately".[10] Works which could render a fairly good income became popular. Not only books, other forms of art like drama, music etc., could command a price in the market. Art thus became a highly remunerative activity. Artists in turn started to look upon the market for getting remuneration for their works. Actually, from 18th century onwards, many artists began to earn fairly good amount of money by selling their works. In England, Alexander Pope for example, could earn as much as 4,000 pounds each out of his *Iliad* and *Odyssey* and Dr. Johnson could earn 1,575 pounds. Around this time painters could charge 50 pounds for a portrait and musicians ten guineas for playing privately[11]. Thus artists could free themselves from the clutches of the patrons and could earn fairly good amount of money from the market for their works. However, artistic products became some sort of commodities and many writers transformed themselves as traders instead of artists.

A far more significant development in the growth of culture is the invention of photography with which the pictures of any object or activity can be taken. The discovery of the principle of persistent vision in combination with the invention of photography, created a plethora of developments in the realm of art and culture. With these discoveries and inventions the possibility for reproducing copies of any kind of work of art and the emergence of new forms of art, like motion pictures were in the anvil. Television which is a further development of these inventions was soon to emerge. The application of all those inventions for artistic creation involves high cost. Naturally people with money alone are able to enter in the creation of artistic works by relying on those technological possibilities. In turn, production of art became a commercial proposition and commodification of art became a total reality with works of art coming out on factory lines. Apparently, what market could fetch became the primary motive for producing works of art.

Instead of conceding the primacy of technological advancement in the evolution of culture industry, the Marxist line of thinking is to look upon the socio-economic development as the prime mover in the evolution of culture industry. According to Marx "it is not the consciousness of man that determines their being, but on the contrary, their social being that determines their consciousness".[12] To Adorno and Horkheimer, the path finders of culture industry, its emergence "is not the result of a law of movement in technology, as such but of its function of today's economy".[13] The possibility for producing cultural goods as mass-marketable commodities would not have arisen but for the Fordist variety of capitalism which encompasses mass production and mass consumption. As Steinert enjoins "without the latter, the above mentioned media would never have been invented (and if they had, they would have remained mere technical experiments-nothing more than curiosities)".[14] Raymond Williams also disregards cultural determinism and concurs socially determined technology as the prime mover.[15] Apparently, the decisive changes in capitalism which occurred during the 20th century has resulted in the emergence of cultural industry in a big way.

Whether it was a socially determined evolution or technologically created process, culture industry became a regular economic activity operating like that of any other commercial venture with the functioning of marketing, production and distribution as its regular features. The stage corresponds to what Hesmondalgh terms 'complex professional' era of cultural production[16]. Gathering, processing, and selling of culture has become a source of employment, not only to artists but also to a host of people. Capital investment in various cultural industries runs into hundreds of billion dollars. People in turn spend a portion of their consumer expenditure on various cultural products, and expenditure on such items has become part of the standard of living.

From Culture Industry to Cultural Industries

Far reaching changes have thus taken place in the realm of art and culture. Many forms of art have been coming out as commodities on regular assembly lines. However, practically nobody seems to have undertaken any serious study in the matter except perhaps to speak of the commodification of art as some Marxist writers did earlier. It was the turn of two German scholars Theodor Adorno and Horkheimer Max of the Frankfurt School to coin the term culture industry and make a study for the first time in the matter.

They introduced the term culture industry in a book of their own entitled *Dialectic of Enlghtenment* published in 1944. The term figures in the form "Culture Industry; Enlightenment as Mass Deception" as the heading to *Chapter* 6 of the book. The authors had a utopian idea about culture as a channel capable of creating an idealized form of life. But unfortunately, it has been converted as a commodity, which can be bought and sold in the market like any other product. Culture and industry which move in different directions coalesced into one resulting in the emergence of an industry producing cultural goods as regular commodities on factory lines. While appearing as a commodity under industrial system, culture also has debased itself as entertainment art. As they put it" with the cheapness of mass produced luxury goods and its compliments, the universal swindle, a change in the character of the art commodity itself is coming about".[17] Art became a pure mercantile commodity that simply responds to demand. As Barbero enjoins, "what remained of art was little more than its shell".[18]

However, when Adorno and Horkheimer wrote, television was only in its infancy. Internet was not yet born. The two scholars were not able to comprehend the future course of developments in the field of culture with these inventions. What they did was to express their anguish at the deplorable condition in which culture has landed itself by adopting industrial and commercial yardsticks. At the same time, culture itself is a hetrogenous phenomenon, encompassing different activities. The logic under which each branch of culture operates on industrial lines may not be similar to each other. Accordingly, some other scholars believe that the term culture industry in the singular form is unsuitable to explain the manner under which different categories of cultural activities operate on industrial lines. They have therefore substituted the plural term cultural industries in the place of culture industry. In the opinion of Hesmondhalgh "the term cultural industries signals an awareness of the problems but a refusal to simplify assessment and explanation".[19] Moreover, Adorno and Horkheimer give the impression that the cultural world has made a total surrender to the dictates of industrial capitalism. What they give expression amounts also to a totally pessimistic picture about the future of culture. Taking the cue from Morin, Barbero maintains that "the division of labour and technological mediation of the culture industry are not incompatible with artistic creation".[20] Their pessimistic assertion that something industrial cannot be art is untenable. Instead, some other authors maintain that the artists are able to retain certain amount of autonomy not withstanding the emergence of culture industry, and that the emergence of an industry around culture needs not be construed as a disaster. Furthermore, culture industry as such is a contested one on account of the difficulty of defining culture. Notwithstanding the improvements made by the critics like Miege, Morin etc., on what Adorno and Horkheimer have written, the conceptual formulation of the former holds good in spite of the shortcomings. The rationale is somewhat similar as in the case of the term entrepreneur. The term entrepreneur as coined by Cantillon remains intact as a key concept, despite the fact that entrepreneur remains as an elusive figure. Similarly, the singular term culture industry can convey the full implication of culture in its industrial complexion. However, Adorno and Horkheimer on their part have not explored the implication of cultural industry in full, except perhaps to draw a pessimistic picture of its fall as a "cathedral dedicated to elevated pleasure".[21] After all, the adoption of mechanical process and factory line can throw open the field of art and culture for further progress and improvement. Nor have they uncovered the complexion of the industry which is still growing since they introduced the concept. In the words of Steinert," the book maintains its poise only through its framework of academic style and poetic image and through the elegance of its complicated shifts in thought, aided by its lofty distance from the subject-matter".[22]

Another serious defect of their thinking seems to be their unwillingness to accommodate commodification and the subsequent processing of culture under factory line. As mentioned earlier, material concerns have also a say in the creative works. Even Marx was prepared to accommodate commodification as a fait accompli. He has conceded that capitalist production is applicable to a restricted extent as for example, in the case of joint products like an encyclopaedia.[23] The involvement of technology in the creation of art has, to a large extent altered even the function of art in the case of exhibition. However, technology has introduced the element of cost as a major concern to be faced by the artists for the creation of works of art. Most of the artists do not have access to costly means of production for which technology cannot be blamed. Adorno and Horkheimer do not seem to have made any attempt to examine any of those issues which have cropped up with large scale technological involvement in so far art and culture are concerned.

Notwithstanding the credibility of culture industry as a concept, terms like entertainment industry, leisure industry, knowledge industry, media industry, consciousness industry etc., are used by authors from different countries to delienate the activities falling within the ambit of culture industry. The term leisure industry stands for activities like sports and tourism along with many of the products of the regular cultural industry. However, the term culture industry connotes the activities like that of the creation of works of art containing cathartic elements. Information industries give prominence to information in the modern period and not to any cultural aspect. The US business circles give prominence to the term entertainment industry which includes not only many components of cultural industry proper, but also craft based industries like jewellery, fashion, furniture, design etc. Apparently, it cannot give full expression to the products falling within the contours of culture industry. Media industry is a term frequently interchanged with the concept of culture industry, but the term media industry is having its own problems of definition, as in the case of culture industry. Furthermore, media is concerned more with the conveyance of contents than with the contents per se. The focus of attention of culture industry is to give importance to both the aspects. The term consciousness industry stands for cultural creations undertaken by technicians rather than by artists for making financial gains. These concepts do not by themselves convey the full implications of culture industry. On the other hand, the term culture industry can in some way or other encompass media, entertainment, information and leisure. The term can certainly invoke as Hesmondhalgh enjoins "the relationship between culture and economics, texts and industry, meaning and function".[24] Needless to say, the relationship between culture and economics forms the axis around which culture industry revolves.

Implications

Culture industry comprises a wide variety of activities relating to culture and art. The growth of an industry around cultural activity creates an altogether new situation in so far as art is concerned. As already stated, art does not involve the creation of any material product. The word creation rather than production is applied in the case of artistic works. It relies more on creative faculties rather than material means in their creation. Nevertheless, artists have to rely on material means produced by economic activities for their subsistence. Apparently, economic activities provide the base for cultural activities and culture forms the superstructure. The base—superstructure dichotomy introduced by Marxist scholars serves as a conceptual formulation for understanding the relations between the two.

Prima facie, the norms governing economic activities may not be applicable in the case of artistic creations. In fact, art is regarded as an autonomous activity operating with its own norms independent of material considerations. However, when art acquires the characteristics of an industry by applying advanced technology which calls for high cost, it becomes more of an economic activity rather than a cultural activity. A situation somewhat similar to an invasion of the superstructure by the base becomes the outcome The so called distinction between the base and superstructure may get blurred under such a situation. In turn, artistic autonomy becomes the casuality. Significantly, as mentioned earlier the erosion of autonomy was the main anxiety of Adorno. Needless to say, economic norms which guide industrial activity assume crucial role in guiding cultural industry. Nevertheless, according to many authors artists are provided with relative autonomy in comparison to other workers in producing cultural goods even under industrial system.

Productivity of labour forms an important yardstick around which the entire process of industrial activities revolves. Productivity stands for increase in output at low unit cost resulting in maximum gain to the capitalist producer. Under capitalist mode of production, an entrepreneur will employ additional labourer, if the marginal revenue product is higher than the amount of remuneration payable to that labourer. Application of such a norm is sure to relegate the artist to the level of a mere labourer. On the other hand, as Kant maintains artists are supposed to be a class of free labour, as opposed to the ordinary labour who serves the role of mercenary labour. Apparntly, when cultural goods are produced on factory lines, artists alo would be compelled to seek employment like the ordinary labour.

As in the case of ordinary labour, they are bound to produce goods in such a way as to fetch maximum return to the capitalist employer. Original and creative works of art get neither recognition nor proper remuneration. Lamenting on the deplorable conditions of genuine artists, Marx wrote "Milton who wrote *Paradise Lost* for 5 pounds was not a productive worker.... On the other hand. the worker who turns out stuff for the factory owner becomes a productive worker".[25] Needless to say, artists are compelled to produce works of cheap and inferior quality.

With the so-called commodification of art, the nature of the products also undergoes serious change. Works of art are supposed to be unique in nature which cannot be reproduced or repeated. Factory lines of production demand mass production and standardization. As already stated, the technological advancement for reproduction of the original constitutes one of the important facilitating factors which paved the way for the growth of cultural industry. With the possibility for reproduction more number of copies can be produced at minimum cost by which mass audience can be served with the reprint at a very low price in comparison with the original. Producers are thus able to increase their earnings by reproducing copies of the original at cheap rate. Newspapers, films, books and various kinds of culture industry thrive by taking advantage of this pssiblity. However, it will be difficult to distinguish the original from the duplicate. Furthermore, the uniqueness and aura of art become the main casuality. At the same time, instead of producing works of quality, cheap and entertainment opiates are only produced.

When production is carried under factory line with minute division of labour it can also lead to what is known as alienation of the product from the producer. Any work of art contains a close personal relationship between the artist and his product. When works are turned out as a joint product as in the case of an encyclopedia this relationship becomes weak. With minute division of labour of the Fordist model, even the semblance of relationship between the producer and the product totally disappears. The producers themselves may not be in a position to understand as to what the nature of the product is. The situation is somewhat similar to the observation of Brȩcht that "I have no idea of what rice is, I know only its price ".[26] In other words, price becomes the dominating factor in controlling the whole process. As Fischer aptly adds "we speak of price trends, stock exchange prices, and by so doing we acknowledge the inhuman autonomous movement of objects, a movement that carries human beings along as a stream carries twigs of wood".[27] Marketing which thus caries human beings becomes inevitable on account the investment of huge amounts of capital for the production of cultural products on factory lines. Marketing is undertaken not merely as a measure to recoup the cost, but to gain maximum profit. Accordingly, various marketing strategies and techniques designed to increase the returns are evolved. An important marketing strategy is to promote entertainment art with an eye to attract the attention of the consumers. The promotion of entertainment art in turn, leads to various undesirable consequences. The purpose of art per se is not merely to entertain people but also to represent serious issues of real life. Entertainment as such introduces only make-believe situations. When make to believe situations are carried to the extreme level, it can create some sort of emotional vacuum which can turn out to be a threat to the progress of the society. Thus culture industry can lead to various undesirable consequences.

Another step in the marketing is to rely on advertisement. Advertisement itself is a form of art or art as suitably modified for making advertisement. Advertisement can create an awareness in the minds of people about any product. However, in most cases it creates a false impression or illusion rather than presenting the correct picture as a newspaper reported as far back as 1859 that "advertising is resorted for the purpose of introducing inferior articles in the market".[28] Advertisements leads to the extreme level of creating an addiction among the consumers. Huge amounts of money are being spent regularly on advertisement during recent years. Producers of art also vie with one another for selling their goods by lavishly spending more on advertisement. However, in the case of enterprises like newspaper and television, advertisement forms the main source of income rather than as expenditure. In another sense, advertisers function like the patrons of the past in propping up the culture industry. However, in both cases the burden of the amount so spent on advertisement is conveniently shifted to the consumers.

In sum, what transpires in culture industry is the triumph of invested capital. Mass production, oriented to serve the needs of a mass society is the yard stick. Conspicuous consumption leads to conspicuous production. In the case of art, what is produced is only mass art which satisfies the demands of mass consumers. Artistic creativity gets only secondary importance.

Distinctive Features of the Industry

Culture industry, undertaking the production of culture on factory lines has certain distinctive features of its own. Unlike other industries, the element of risk is very high in culture industry. Risk arises mainly because of the uniqueness of cultural products. Very often, standardization with formatting the star system is adopted as away out to face the uncertainty in the market. In turn the earnings of super stars rise disproportionately higher than that of the ordinary actors. Adherance to the formulas which have proved successful in the box office, as is usually practiced in film industry is being followed in TV also.

Another distinctive feature relates to the wide variation in the cost of production between the original and the duplicate. While the cost is very high in the case of originals, duplicates can be produced at very low cost. This variation which has contributed much to the emergence of an industry around culture has far reaching implications on the marketing in a culture industry like television.

Cultural commodities are basically public goods. Their value will not diminish with continuous use. Instead, they will remain intact for any length of time. On account this reason, artificial scarcity is being created on the supply.

Complexion of the Industry

Art itself is a complex phenomenon. Culture industry encompasses a wide variety of artistic activities which are commodified through assembly line and marketd as commercial goods. However, what exactly are the activities which can be included in the culture industry remains a doubtful proposition on account of the difficulty in demarcating the boundaryline of culture. As Steinert puts, "In order to understand culture industry, we must take an active interest in all its products; from Barbie to basketball, from John Cage to the comic book, from Geothe to garden gnome, from home appliances to Hundertwasser, from classical music festivals to the cinema, from Macbeth to mass marathons, from sports stadiums to strip clubs, from tourism to talk shows and from Westerns to Wagner".[29] Apparently, a wide variety of activities and the products thereof fall within the fold of culture industry. Throsby proposes a model with the locus of origin of creative ideas as the centre of culture industry with more and more other inputs, combining to produce a wider range of products. On the basis of such a model, music, dance, theatre, literature, the visual arts, the crafts, and including newer forms of products such as video art, computer and multimedia art and so on form the core of the industry[30]. The next category consists of those industries whose output qualifies as a cultural commodity but with lower proportion of cultural content in comparison with the core sector. According to him, this group can be thought of as including book and magazine publishing, television and radio, newspaper and film. In all these cases, as he puts, "both cultural and non-cultural goods and services are produced side by side".[31] According to authors like

Hesmondhalgh, the boundaries of culture industry can be extended further and include certain activities which lay outside the proper cultural sphere, but some of whose products have some degree of cultural content. Advertisement, tourism and architectural designs form the prominent among those industries. Among them advertisement is in fact, treated as a core cultural industry as creative input is of crucial importance in advertisement. Similarly, tourist marketing is impregnated with cultural segments. Architectural designs embody qualitative elements on a significant scale. Hesmondalgh also divides culture industries as those belonging to the core and periphery. According to him, the core comprises advertising and marketing, broadcasting consisting of radio and television industries, including their cable, satellite and digital forms; film industry, internet industries, music industries, print and electronic publishing, video and computer games. Though the periphery is concerned with the production of texts, they rely on semi-industrial or non-industrial methods. Theatres, art exhibition etc., fall under this category. In addition, the trend is for the commodification of sports, tourism etc. They can therefore be included within the borderline of culture industry.[32]

Television as a Constituent Unit of the Culture Industry

Television has shot into prominence and assumed new dimensions since Adorno and Horkheimer conceptualized culture industry. Television is a communicative medium through which texts are telecast. The texts containing cultural contents are produced with the help of other inputs and telecast through technological means. Television has naturally a claim to be treated as a unit of culture industry. Since culture industry is a contested term on account of the difficulty of defining culture, there is some ambiguity regarding the position of television among the various kinds of culture industry. As mentioned earlier, Throsby does not assign television a place within the core sector of culture industry. According to him, television holds a rank among the second category of cultural industry. The reason seems to be the inclusion of news and instructional themes as an integral part among the programmes. However, the roots and formats of these kinds of programmes are also cultural in origin. No wonder, almost all the other authors assign a place to television within the core sector of culture industry.

As in the case of any other branch of culture industry, television concentrates on entertainment rather than on other cultural formats. It was the undue importance assigned to entertainment which has brought the wrath of the authors of the Frankfurt School and other critics on television. However, entertainment as such forms an important cultural activity. As Altschull puts "it has been part of human experience since the beginning of time. Life without entertainment, private and public is impossible to imagine".[33] In fact, as Postman concurs "television has made entertainment the natural format for the representation of all experiences".[34] Nevertheless, in most cases, sub-standard entertainment programmes are being transmitted by television channels for making popular appeal under the dictates of commercial considerations.

Television is a new technology through which all forms of cultural products can be telecast. Being a technological device, it is a very costly one. It has grown as an economic venture from the very beginning. Economic norms have a decisive say in the functioning of television. However, as in the case of any cultural industry, determination of output is a problematic issue in the case of television. The problem assumes crucial importance, because it is a novel form of culture industry through which all forms of art and other programmes can be relayed, very often in the live form. What is relayed functions to a large extent like the sunlight on the earth which is a free good shared by all. Similarly, television programmes can be viewed by people in any part of the world with the help of an antenna. What is consumed or viewed alone can be construed as the output. How to measure the output naturally becomes a complicated issue.

The competition which the industry faces also becomes a complicated one. Different channels produce programmes and relay them simultaneously. Which programme is better than any other programme is the question? Different categories of people are employed in television. Similarly, television relays not merely artistic products per se, but also other products like day-to-day events, scientific information. Can we regard them also as cultural programmes? What is the role of each category is another problem.

In short, television, an important branch of the culture industry differs very much from any other industry on various aspects. Complexion of the products, modus operandi of marketing, labour market behaviour, consumer response to the products, etc., are some of the areas noted for marked differences between television and any other ordinary industry. Before probing into the details of those differences with reference to television in India, how an industry could emerge around television, and its economic significance would be delineated, as a starting point.

NOTES AND REFERENCES

1. Throsby, David (2001). *Economics and Culture,* Cambridge University Press, p. 3.
2. Harris, Marvin (1979). *Cultural Materialism,* Norfolk, Random Press, p. 47.
3. Vasquez Adolf Sanchez (1973). *Art and Society: Essays in Marxist Aesthetics,* London, Merlin Press, p. 192.
4. Irwin, Edman (1939). *Art and the Man: A Short Introduction to Aesthetics,* NewYork, W.W. Norton.
5. Joyce, Carey (1958). *Art and Reality,* Cambridge University Press.
6. Ernst, Fischer (1959). *The Necessity of Art: A Marxist Approach,* Penguin Books, p. 8.
7. Jacquetta, Hawkes and Leonard, Woolley (1963). *History of Mankind: Culture and Scientific Development Vol. 1 Pre-history and the Beginnings of Civilisation,* London, George Allen and Urwin, p. 8.
8. Marx, Karl (1958). *Le Capital,* Reproduced in Marx, Engels on Literature and Art; Moscow, Progressive Publication, p. 46.
9. Osborne, Harold (1968). *Aesthetics and Art Theory: An Historical Introduction,* London, Longman Green & Co., p. 15.
10. Eisenstein, Elizabeth L. (1979). *Printing Press as the Agent of Change,* Cambridge, University Press, p. 153.

11. John, Pick (1986). *Managing the Art: A British Experience*, London, Rhingold Publishing Company Ltd., p. 16.
12. Marx, Karl. *Preface to the Critique of Political Economy*, Reproduced in Marx, Engles, *op. cit.*, p. 41.
13. Adorno, T.W. and Horkheimer. *Max Culture Industry: Enlightenment as Mass Deception*, Reproduced in Steinert Heinz (2003), *Culture Industry*, Cambridge Polity Press.
14. Heinz, Steinert (2003). *Culture Industry*, Translated by Sally Ann Spencer, Cambridge, Polity Press, p. 76.
15. Raymond, Williams (1975). *Television: Technology and Cultural Form*, London, Routledge, p. 13.
16. Hesmondhalgh, David (2000). *The Cultural Industries*, London, Sage Publications. p. 50. In fact, Williams had indicted of three stages in the evolution of culture industry. They are: patronage, market professional and corporate professional eras Hesmondalgh substituted the term 'complex professional' instead of corporate professional.
17. Adorno T.W. and Horkheimer Max (1977). *op. cit.*, p. 376 (reproduced in Curran, James (ed) *Mass Communication and Society*, London, Open University, p. 376.
18. Martin, Barbero Jesus (1993). *Communication Culture and Hegemony*, New Delhi, Sage, p. 43.
19. Hesmondhalgh, David (2000). *op. cit.*, p. 17.
20. Martin, Barbero Jesus (1993). *op. cit.*, p. 54.
21. Adorno, T.W. and Horkheimer Max. *op. cit.*, p. 365.
22. Heinz, Steinert (2003). *op. cit.*, p. 19.
23. Marx, Karl. *Theories of Surplus Value*, Part 1. p. 410-41, reproduced in Marx, Engles *op. cit.*, p. 145.
24. Hesmondhalgh (2000). *op. cit.*, p. 14.
25. Marx, Karl. *Theories of Surplus Value*, reproduced in Marx Engles, *op. cit.*, p. 144.
26. Brecht, Bertold (1990). *Poems and Songs from the Plays*, London, Macmillan. p. 101.
27. Fischer, Ernst (1959). *op. cit.*, p. 82.
28. Williams Raymond quotes the passage from a newspaper of 1859. See Williams Raymond; "Advertising the Magic System" in Simon Diving (ed.) (1993). *The Cultural Studies*, London, Routledge, p. 324.
29. Heinez, Steinert (2003) *op. cit.*, p. 12.
30. David, Throsby (2001). *Economics and Culture*, Cambridge, University Press, p. 113.
31. *Ibid.*
32. Hesmondhalgh, David (2000). *op. cit.*, pp. 12-14.
33. Altschull, Herbert J. (1995). *The Media and Public Policy: Agents of Power*, London, Longman, p. 127.
34. Altschull Herbert, J. (1995). *op. cit.*, quotes from Postman, see p. 128.

3

Growth of TV as an Industry

Technological inventions have been able to make far reaching changes in the life of man. However, the inventions which have made changes at a very short period are few in numbers. Television is one among such inventions. Ever since its introduction in 1936, it has revolutionised the life of man far beyond recognition. It has grown as a distinct category of the culture industry engaging in the production of a wide variety of cultural products and services. How it has grown as an industry since its inception and its further development during the last half a century form, the theme of this Chapter.

The growth of television as an industry can be thought in terms of improvement in technology. As Bignell puts "from the earliest mechanical devices for broadcasting pictures, through the invention of cable television, the history of television is driven by technological innovation".[1] However, technological innovations call for financial resources on a large scale for its emergence as an industry which in turn relies on organizational structure for marketing the products. In the case of television, the progressive introduction of various cultural genres forms another side of its emergence as an industry.

Beginnings of TV

As in the case of many inventions, no single person can be credited with having invented television. A number of personalities hailing from different parts of the world have actually contributed to the invention and development of television. Among them Paul Nipkov, John Logie Baird, Vladimir K. Zworykin, David Sarnoff, Phillo Fransworth are the prominent personalities. Works for the development of television had simultaneous origin on parallel lines in different parts of the world during the closing decades of nineteenth century itself. All the initial ventures were experimental in nature till the outbreak of the First World War. Credit goes to Paul Nipkov, a German for transmitting pictures through a mechanical system using scanning disc in 1884. Images could be transmitted through the scanning disc by using a series of wires between the disc and the receiver. Pictures were scanned by punctuating holes in the disc and rotating the disc by which the spectators could get the impression of a continuation of the events as per the principle of persistent vision. According to it, the spectators can get the impression of a sequence of events when a series of still pictures are exhibited one after another in quick succession. Nipkov's device was a crude one which lacked many components to relay the clear picture of an activity or event. However, his invention was a starting point which could be used for continued experimentation by scientists in many countries. It was the turn of Phillo Farnsworth to perfect the successful electronic transmission. He started experimentation on electronic transmission of pictures from his schooldays in 1921 when he was only a 15 year old boy. He pursued his work with the help of some of his friends and by 1930 he could secure patent rights for the television system and receiving system perfected by him. Around this time Zworykin, a Russian immigrant who had made some experiments before the Revolution was also on the work for developing an electronic television system. Zworykin succeeded in inventing iconoscope, a kind of television pick up tube on which the experiments started from the early 1920s could be perfected during 1930s. He entered into a patent dispute with Farnsworth which was adjudged in favour of the latter. Subsequently, Farnsworth entered into a licensed agreement for $1 million with Radio Corporation America (RCA) by which he collaborated with Zworykin who was employed there.[2] With the two pioneers in its roll, RCA under the stewardship of Sanroff could complete the TV system by 1936.

While experiments were thus going on in the US, Great Britain was also the scene of a parallel research with John Logie Baird as the leading light. During the initial stages of his endeavours he was not getting practically any financial support from any agency. However by 1932, he made a working agreement with BBC by which he could get modest financial support from BBC to pursue his experimentations on TV. In spite of the break through made by him on various aspects of TV, doubts were raised regarding the quality of his products and in consequence BBC made a parallel agreement with EMI company which was linked with RCA of US, for the development of TV. The agreement with Baird came to an end by 1934 before Baird could perfect the system and Baird has remained as an embittered man. Development of both the systems of TV were pursued and on 2nd November, 1936, the BBC could inaugurate its TV broadcast for which it relied more on EMI system. "Chinese jugglers, American dancers, news reels and speeches, and especially composed song "Television" sung by Adele Dixon were interesting items of the initial programming".[3] It is surprising that Britain had a march ahead of US in arranging the public transmission, though America had a lead in the research on TV. "The American tardiness", as Ward puts "was the result of patent disputes, problems of agreeing technical standards with the Federal Communications Commission (FCC) and the unwillingness of RCA and the network to rush into a development which had no clear commercial potential and which might affect the lucrative returns from radio".[4]

Nevertheless, experimentation with TV was in full swing in the US. Some of the leading companies were actively engaged in the development of TV and in fact, nearly seventeen experimental stations were involved in exhibitions which were held here and there. Finally, TV was formally inaugurated during the World Fair held in New York on April 1939. President Roosevelt of the US, who opened the fair, appeared in the TV while inaugurating the fair. In turn, NBC to which RCA was associated, started to broadcast regularly, for a duration of two hours a week. As the year wore on programmes like opera, comedy, music, puppet shows and kitchen demonstrations appeared on TV. In the meanwhile, legal sanction was accorded for the continuance of TV on an experimental basis.[5]

The out break of the War resulted in the suspension of further expansion of TV. Nevertheless, TV has become a reality in the USA, UK and a few European countries like Germany. The National Television System Committee which was formed in the US to settle the standards fixed 525 scanning lines and thirty complete scanning of the picture each second as the norm. License was given to as many as 12 channels in 1941 and TV on commercial lines started to function from that date. However, only six channels were actually operating in the US during the War period. All of them were in the private sector. On the other hand, TV was a state monopoly with BBC operating as the only channel in Great Britain. When the War started there were only about 10,000 television receiving sets in the US.[6] On the other hand, as many as 20,000-25,000 households were owning TV sets in London alone. In UK and Germany TV programmes were suspended during the War period on account of the fear of aerial attacks.

Introduction of Colour TV

When the War ended there was a rush for station licenses in the US and FCC in turn issued licenses to 30 stations in 1946 itself. It increased to 109 by 1948. When new licenses were given complaints about signal interference began to surface and consequently there was a freeze again in 1948. The freeze was lifted in 1952 after distributing channel frequencies between VH and UHP channels. About two-hundred and forty-two channels were reserved for non-commercial purposes comprising mostly for educational programmes. The stations operating in 1948 were able to cover 64 cities and metropolitan areas and as a result of which nearly 87 million people could view programmes from at least one television station. Simultaneously, there was a spurt in the sale of TV sets. As many as 73,55,000 TV sets were sold in 1950. By 1955, nearly

55 per cent of the houses were equipped with at least one television set.[7]

One notable development was improvement in technology. The pick up tube invented by Zworykin, known as kinescope, was the earliest instrument used for taking the pictures. Since it lacked technical perfection, other kinds of pick up tubes like orthicon pick up tube, plumbicon tube, and videocon camera were invented subsequently. However, the most important development was the introduction of colour TV. A primitive form of colour television had been introduced by John. L. Baird in 1928. Though further experimentations were made since then, colour was reserved for the future in the wake of the outbreak of the Second World War. When the War came to an end many companies were in the fray for making colour television instruments with two companies, CBSand RCA in a neck to—neck competition in the run for perfecting colour TV. In the first round CBS won the race, by winning FCC nod to introduce their colour system in 1951. However, after an initial hesitation FCC revoked its earlier license and approved the RCA colour system in 1953. With this approval RCA could maintain its monopoly position for a long period. As a result of the approval of the colour system, sale of colour TV sets began to swell, though the price of a colour set was as high as $1,000 in those days. The number of colour sets sold which was only 20,000 in 1955, increased to 26,94,000 by 1965. By 1972, the sale of colour sets surpassed that of the monochrome sets; the actual number being 79,08,000 colour sets against 56,00,000 monochrome sets. Sale of TV sets reached saturation by 1975/76. As high as 97 per cent of the homes were provided with one TV set. Of them 79 per cent were provided with colour set.[8]

Video Tape

Another important technological invention which facilitated the making of television programmes more effective was video tape. With this invention, programmes could be recorded and replayed or relayed with the tape. Continuity of the programmes and location shooting could be made easily with video tape. Since its invention in 1950s, video tapes were increasingly used side by side with films for the making of pictures for TV. Electronic newsgathering was another invention which made TV more effective and natural. Live shooting from air of the football stadiums, court house boats and other day to day developments could be made from different locations.

Cable Television

The invention of cable system is another important development which was instrumental for the further growth of the industry. When television was in its infancy it was difficult to get the magic pictures relayed from the transmitting stations even with the help of the best antennas then available. Very often, television signals moving in high altitude were obstructed by the mountains and tall buildings. Low lying areas were thus precluded from the vicinity of television signals. As a way out, Community Antenna Television (CATV) was installed in areas which were not able to receive television signals. The system is somewhat akin to household antennas which pick up the signals relayed from TV stations and pass on to the receiving set. Similarly, the television signals received by big antennas are amplified by complex electronic equipments and sent into the cables which in turn carry them to TV sets in the neighbouring localities. With large antennas mounted on hill tops or elevated places, signals can reach low lying areas. Cables can receive signals from different channels and send them to the receiving sets. The transcontinental hookup with ability to carry pictures was completed by 1951.[9] The people who took connections can select any programme from the cable thus connected. Cable can connect programmes from as many as 100 stations or more. However, they could not cover the oceans and intercontinental connections. With the invention of satellite linking system, programmes from anywhere in the world can be retransmitted through the cable with which the consumers are provided with TV programmes for every twenty four hours a day.

Satellite Link with TV

During the formative days of TV, stations were spacially distributed in such a way as to make TV programmes accessible to the people living in all parts of the US. However, it was very costly for the channels to prepare programmes for each station. They felt that a central source for programmes would be helpful to a number of local stations. As a starting point, they connected the stations through coaxial cables. Thus, micro wave system, which facilitates the coast to coast network broadcasts, connected with the cables, came into being by 1951. The national networks, were able to link a large number of stations distributed in various parts of the US around this time. Since the networks were companies engaging in various kinds of cultural business particularly in the radio broadcasting field, they could do it in quick succession. However, such networks required amplifiers, microwaving studios in addition to the cables to connect the stations.

The invention of satellites solved most of these problems as satellites can reach long distance without encountering any hindrance. As a matter fact, one satellite can cover about one third of the earth. Earlier satellites operated like a mirror reflecting the images. Later on satellites equipped with their own transmitters and receivers or transponders as they are called, were invented. They pick up the signals from earth and retransmit them back to the earth. The communication satellites are stationed some 22,300 miles away from the equator and they rotate at the same speed as that of the earth. A satellite can hold signals from several television channels. The programmes received through the satellites are in turn transmitted to the households by cable TV. With the further sophistication of satellites, several million homes are able to take their television signals directly from satellites through a reception dish, bypassing local stations and cables.[10] People with cable or satellite reception can now view channels that feature nothing but sports, religious ceremonies, rock music, movies, children shows, etc., as they like. Many of these programmes can be tuned at any time of the day. At the same time, signals beamed through the satellites can be received in any part of the world. TV has therefore become an international or trasnational phenomenon defying national boundaries. In a sense, television with its transnational broadcasting facilities has turned out to be the sustaining force behind the ongoing process of globalization.

Organization of TV

In the US, where brisk experimentation in the making of TV was taking place before the outbreak of Second World War, it emerged in a big way as pure commercial activity soon after the War. As already stated, there was a spurt in the sale of home TV sets. Similarly there was a big expansion in the number of broadcasting stations. The number which was only 30 in 1946 went up to 976 by 1977; with most them making huge amouts of profit. The stations were spatially distributed in such a way as to make them accessible to people all over the country. Taking advantage of the emerging situation, businessmen began to look upon TV as a handy sales promotion instrument on account of its capacity for reaching large number of people situated in far away places. In turn, they came forward with large advertisements in the TV or even to sponsor programmes. What they wanted for these purposes was a large size of audience. Under such circumstances national television networks were established so that large number of audience could be attracted for their programmes and the local commercial stations were connected as affiliates to the national net works. Networks like RCA, Blue Mount etc. had come into existence for the development of radio. Apparently, the system of networks was in the field much before the appearance of television. In fact, television was developed as a broadcasting system mainly with the financial and technical backing of the networks like RCA. Naturally, TV also adopted the model of radio network. Three national networks viz. the NBC, CBS and ABC were organized in the US during the formative days of television on the model of radio networks. The networks render three basic services to their affiliates. First, they purchase or produce programmes and provide them to their affiliates. Second, they sell commercial time to the national advertisers and in turn allot certain portion of advertisement revenue to their affiliates. Third, they facilitate technical interconnections to the affiliates. During those days, the networks were the source for about sixty-five per cent of the programmes of the local stations. The local stations on their part, prepare local news and locally oriented programmes needed for them. The networks were very profit making concerns. Since the preparation of a programme is a costly business, all the channels may not be able to produce programmes of their own. Such stations secure the programmes through a system known as syndication. It was a system by which newspapers used to lease out publication rights of messages and other programmes. Syndication system of the same model was adopted by the TV also. Local TV stations could secure their off-network rerun programmes and movie and many of their public service announcements and educational features through syndication.[11] In addition to the affiliates of the networks, there are a large number of independent stations whose number was stated to be around 250 accounting for about 15 per cent of the total by 1970s. They prepare their own programmes and broadcast them. They also rely on syndication system for the supply of some of their own programmes. Most of them manage to thrive in spite of the competition from the networks.

Apart from those stations operating purely as commercial enterprises for making a profit, as many as 300 public television stations meant for education were also licensed in 1954, soon after the lifting of the ban on the licensing of stations. Actually, certain channel frequencies were reserved for them as it was felt that the commercial stations would not be interested to broadcast educational programmes. They function mainly for educational purposes. They are non-profit organizations which rely on philanthropies, state and federal government and their audiences for financial support.[12] However the funding for PBS has been very inadequate in the US. In the early 1980s the per capita expenditure on public broadcasting has been only 50 to 60 cents against $18 in UK, $22 in Canada, $10 in Japan and so on.[13] They telecast some excellent programmes on various themes. However with only less than 5 per cent of the total audience in the market, PBS does not command a mass audience.[14]

Unlike the private profit making enterprise pattern of the US, TV was organized in Great Britain, as a public sector undertaking from its very inception BBC, a public sector undertaking started in 1923 for preparing and telecasting radio programmes was eventually entrusted with the additional responsibility of developing television also. Significantly, as mentioned earlier, it was BBC which conducted the first successful public broadcasting of television in 1936. A license fee collected from the owners of the domestic TV sets forms the main source of finance and not advertisement. In 1954, Independent Television (ITV) another channel, also in the public sector but independent of BBC was established. It operates like commercial TV by raising its funds from the advertisers. In other countries like France, Canada, Australia, Mexico, and so on TV was organized as public sector enterprises along with private channels. In India also TV was started as a wholly state owned enterprise.

TV and Cultural Production

TV is a technological instrument, designed to address mass audience on a wide range of themes. Cultural themes formed the most important category of the programmes introduced even from the formative days of television. During those days, TV a novelty, had very little experience and technical capability for telecasting interesting themes. It started with limited number of programmes including sports events like football, baseball, tennis, boxing, hockey, news, studio production of plays, musical shows and old movies. In those days, cinema and radio, two other branches of the culture industry were doing brisk business as producers of cultural commodities. Television also followed the footsteps of these industries before emerging as a full-fledged industry. However as Mullan puts, "many television formats and templates were developed in the early experimental years of 1960s and 1970s"[15]. Comedies like "I Love Lucy", variety shows like "Toast of the Town", "Talent Scouts", "Your Show of Shows" were some of the comedies shown then.[16] Many shows relayed on radio moved to television together with the artists. In 1951 NBC, produced one unique programme "Today" which consisted of talk, news and interviews. As television started to display buoyancy, film producers began to apprehend that television would emerge as a serious rival to cinemas. There apprehension was not unfounded. Attendance in cinemas started to fall with the ascendancy of television. In turn, film producers thought of defending themselves by refusing to supply motion pictures to television channels. In the face of such an adverse situation, TV networks also started to produce their own plays. Some of the best dramas ever shown on television like "The Golden Age", "Requiem for a Heavyweight", "Days of Wine and Roses"; all of them focusing on character development and analysis were turned out during those days of hostility of film producers. The hostility of film producers did not last long. As attendance in cinemas continued to fall, film producers reversed their earlier stand, and began to look upon television for preserving their own dwindling hold in the market. A beginning was made when Warner's made an agreement with ABC for the production of 40 one hour programmes based on stories owned by them. By 1957 there were over 100 series on American television using cinematic genres of detective, spy and war spy and war stories.[17] Film companies also came forward to provide cheap but reliable programmes to TV by using materials which were unusable in commercial cinemas. Needless to say, television channels were also benefitted by the changing attitude of film producers.

TV moved to prerecorded dramatic series by the end of 1950s. The "Western" which has been popular on radio was the first genre to be developed like this. There were nearly 30 Westren on prime time by 1959. NBC started airing "Bonaza" in colour on saturday evenings. Its timing was designed in such a way as to promote the sale of colour TV sets sold by RCA, the parent company of NBC. It was one of the popular shows for nearly fifteen years. "Urban Western", another genre with doctor, police, detective and court room shows in which good invariably prevailed over evil became another popular genre.

Situation comedies was another popular theme developed around this period. "All in the Family" was one of the important plays under this category.

Mini-series was another format introduced from mid 1970s. The concept was introduced by the BBC through the presentation of the novels "Forsyte Saga" and "Upstairs Down Stairs" in serial form. The idea was to get people hooked onto the series in the first episode to be followed for the next several evenings. "Roots", "Bacon Hill", "Rich Man Poor Man" etc. were some of the very popular series of this category televised in the US on the basis of the model introduced by BBC.[18]

One of the most important entertainment programmes which became popular from 1960s was soap operas. It was a mini-serial inherited from radio by TV. The name soap opera is derived as soap companies like Procter and Gamble promoted the genre. Soap operas are known as Telenovelas in Latin America where they became very popular.[19] It is appealing to the rich and the poor alike and its central theme revolves around the moral that wealth cannot bring happiness. "Dallas", "Dynasty", "Knots Landing", "Falcon Crest" were some of the important titles exhibited in the US. Soap operas became popular not only in America, but also in Australia, Canada and Western Europe.

A combination of the story line from soap opera, character development from earlier dramas, comedy from sitcom, adventure from police and lawyer shows and so on, became the popular theme since 1980s. The trend setter under this theme was "Hill Street Blues". Other shows like "St Elsewhere", "Miami Vice" were able to catch the attention of the audience. Docudrama is another form of fiction which gained popularity during 1980s. They portray real life situation by bringing historical events in fictional form.

Towards the end of 1980s tabloid news version of newspapers entered as another kind of genre with TV. Rupert Murdoch, the kingpin of tabloid news in newspapers was credited to be the brain behind it in TV also. In his attempt to establish a fourth network, Murdoch's Fox Broadcasting company started to use sex, murder and mayhem in TV entertainment programmes. Other networks also followed his step and introduced real murder scenes and crimes as part of entertainment in TV.

Sports

As seen in the previous chapter, there are many activities which stand in the borderline of culture industry. Sports is one of such activities which has become a popular entertainment since the Industrial Revolution. Sports has also become an attractive programme with television. However, during the formative days of television "a succession of BBC managers had to encourage, cajole and inspire sports administrators to persuade them of the benefits which the new machine could bring".[20] The invention of television recorder was the crucial factor in boosting the popularity of televised athletic events. Eventually, some sort of symbiotic relationship has come into existence between sports and television. In the opinion of an author, "it is also correct to say sports programming is one reason television is the popular medium it is today".[21] To some extent the popularity of football in the US is due to its link with television. Interestingly, NFL football started at $50 million in 1970s, ended at $430 million by mid 1980s. Similarly, the ABC television network paid $225 million for the right to telecast the 1984 Summer Olympics. Other sports like basket ball and base ball became equally revenue yielding activities. Significantly, the bid for baseball went up to $1 billion in 1989.[22]

Quiz which was popular with radio offered greater rewards with TV. However, quiz in television was hit with a scandal in which certain contestants were given the questions in advance. Since then, stricter controls were imposed on quiz programmes. It seems to have reappeared with the entry of reality show, a new format in the scene.

News

News figures as an important item among the programmes of television. Beginnings of news telecast were made as early as 1941. Nevertheless, radio dominated the scene during the Second World War period. On account of the technological limitations, television news could not be presented as an interesting item in those days. Naturally, it could not catch the attention of the audience either. News was also an expensive item. Apparently, television authorities on their part regarded news as some sort of a glorious burden. Since 1947, evening news for fifteen minutes duration became a regular programme with some channels. Meet the Press programme was also introduced in 1947 as an important item. Some of the notable events like the Japanese Peace Treaty (1951), Coronation of Queen Elizabeth (1953) were telecast. Interestingly, the coronation became the biggest event in the television history with as many as 277 million people all over the world watching the event.[23] At a later date, important developments like the landing on the moon, Vietnam War, Watergate scandal etc. were covered by TV. As in the case of the Coronation of Queen Elizabeth, the landing on the moon was another remarkable event in the history of television. In the words of Le Roy, "one hundred and twentyfive million Americans watched on television as Neil Armstrong and Edwin Aldrin Jr landed on the moon in 1969".[24] The news coverage on Vietnam war, portrayed it as a dirty affair with the accusing finger on the US. In fact, in the opinion of an author "the television networks were instrumental in ending the US involvement in Vietnam".[25] During the initial stage, television had adopted most of the news format from radio. It was only later on that TV was able to evolve new techniques and formats for news programme. One technique was to make news as an entertaining item. Interestingly, an advisor to president Reagan is reported to have stated that "we do not have news on television; we have entertainment".[26] Presentation of female news readers in attractive costume was another device adopted for making news more popular. Interestingly, one female news reader went into a legal battle, as she was sacked apparently on account of her less glamorous appearance.[27] Some of the news anchors whose command to hold audience, could easily get an annual salary of $2 million around 1980s.[28] Preparation of news paved the way for the emergence of a class of consultants called news doctors who maintain a watch on the attitude of audience on news. The introduction of portable cameras and video tape recorders by 1960s made television an attractive news medium. Eventually, TV could provide news for much more people than either newspapers or radio. Duration of news for 30 minute was introduced from 1962 onwards. By this time, on the spot relay cover stories could be broadcast on account of further improvement in technology. With the opening of Ted Turner's Cable News Network (CNN), 24 hour news programme has become another reality. His reporting of the Gulf war in 1991, was a landmark in news making programmes by arranging news from both sides.

Challenges to TV

TV, a culture industry fuelled by technology is being challenged from different quarters. However, challenges stemming from the developments in technology form the most important. Video piracy is one among them. Under the threat from video piracy producers find it difficult to safeguard their copyright. Digitalisation of television would create another set of problems to the industry. However, the threat from internet would perhaps be the biggest challenge to the TV system as a whole. In the opinion of McPhail, the role of internet in the information age would be similar to "what the automobile was to the industrial age".[29] Though it has become operational only in 1990s, it is growing at a fast rate. By 2004 there were as many as 202.5 million internet users in the US. More than half the number of internet users are stated to be in the US. It has also spread at a quick pace in Western Europe, China, Japan, Canada, South Korea, and so on. These countries possess technical expertise, financial resources and infrastructural facilities required for internet access. In the opinion of Vinton Serf, one of the leading pioneers in the making of internet television industry is rapidly approaching the same kind of crunch moment that the music industry faced with the arrival of the MP3 player. He predicts further that people would soon be watching the majority of television programmes through the internet and that the revolution could herald the death of the traditional broadcast TV channel in favour of new interactive service.[30]

The threat may not be so serious in the less developed countries as they lack the necessary preconditions for its penetration. Even in the developed nations, the internet reaches only 50 per cent of the population and the average daily use is for about 100 minutes.[31] Moreover internet is an instrument basically structured for use in English language. Not surprisingly, as McPhail enjoins" the internet is both US-centric and English dominated". Actually, for every page on the internet which is non-English, there are at least 100 pages of English text.[32] Apparently, its penetration may not be so quick in the non-English language speaking countries. Nevertheless, TV has to restructure its mode of activities, if at all it is to face the challenge from the internet.

Conclusion

In sum, Television which was only in the experimental stage on the eve of the Second World War, has grown as a gigantic industry within the last sixty years, not only in the US, but in many other countries of the world. The amount of money invested in television channels runs into hundreds of billion dollar. Not only in terms of the amount of capital investment, but also in the volume of employment, it stands foremost as an industry.

NOTES AND REFERENCES

1. Bignell, Jonathan (2004). *An Introduction to Television Studies*, London, Routledge, p. 41.
2. Bittner, John R. (1980). *Broadcasting and Television: An Introduction*, New Jersey, Prentice Hall, p. 90.

3. Bob, Mullan (1997). *Consuming Television*, Oxford, Blackwell Publishers, p. 21.
4. Ken, Ward (1989). *Mass Communication and the Modern World*, London, Macmillan Education, p. 173.
5. Hybels, Saundra and Daria, Ulloth (1978). *Broadcasting An Introduction to Radio and Television*, New York, D. Van Nostrad Company, p. 94.
6. Hybels and Ulloth (1978). *op. cit.*, p. 98.
7. Hybels and Ulloth (1978). *op. cit.*, p. 95.
8. Hybels and Ulloth (1978). *op. cit.*, p. 105.
9. Hybels and Ulloth (1978). *op. cit.*, p. 33.
10. Wilson San Le Roy (1988). *Mass Media and Mass Culture; An Introduction*, New York, Random House, p. 225.
11. James, Harless (1990). *Mass Communication: An Introductory Survey*, Dubuque, US, WmC. Brown Publishers, p. 348.
12. James, Harless (1990). *op. cit.*, p. 291.
13. James, Harless (1990). *op. cit.*, p. 324.
14. Wilson, San Le Roy (1988). *op. cit.*, p. 225.
15. Bob, Mullan (1997). *op. cit.*, p. 109.
16. Hybels and Ulloth (1978). *op. cit.*, p. 109.
17. Ward, Ken (1989). *op. cit.*, p. 184.
18. Wilson San Le Roy (1988). *op. cit.*, p. 204.
19. Singhal, Arvind and Everett, M. Rogers (2000). *India's Communication Revolution*, New Delhi, Sage Publications, p. 90.
20. Steven, Barnett (1998). "Sport" in Smith Anthony (ed.) *Televison an International History*, Oxford University Press, p. 86.
21. James, Harless (1990). *op. cit.*, p. 301.
22. James, Harless (1990). *op. cit.*, p. 303.
23. Bob, Mullan (1997). *op. cit.*, p. 6.
24. Wilson San Le Roy (1988). *op. cit.*, p. 19.
25. Brown Les (1998). "The American Networks" in Smith Anthony (ed.) *op. cit.*, p. 156.
26. Altschull, Herbert J. (1995). *Agents of Power; The Media and Public Policy*, New York, Longman Publishers, p. 124.
27. Wilson San Le Roy (1988). *op. cit.*, p. 215.
28. James, Harless, *op. cit.*, p. 296.
29. McPhail, Thomas L. (2006). *Global Communication: Theories, Stakeholders and Trends*, Oxford, Blackwell Publishers, p. 290.
30. Bobbie, Johnson (2007) in *The Hindu*.
31. Lawrence, Meyer (2006). "Three Scenarios for TV in 2015" in *Communications and Strategies*, June, 2006.
32. McPhail, Thomas L. (2004). *op. cit.*, p. 311.

4

Television in India

Television appeared in India only in 1959 as an experimental measure. Apparently, it has a history of only fiftyone years. Within this short period, it has grown as a major economic activity in which capital investment alone apart from other parameters runs into hundreds of million rupees. The purpose of this chapter is to delineate the growth of TV in India and its economic significance from a historical angle.

Arrival of Television

Television had its beginnings in India with the transmission of a programme for half an hour, as an experimental measure, on 15 September 1959, from a 500 watt transmitter temporarily erected, at the Akashvani Bhavan, Delhi under an UNESCO aided scheme. During the initial stage, the programmes were for a duration of one hour each on Tuesdays and Fridays and were visible only within a range of 25 kilometers around Delhi. In those days, most of the programmes were on informative and educational themes like illustrated talks, interviews, dialogues, discussions, documentary films, plays, kits, puppet shows, dance drama, ballet and light and classical music.[1] The arrival of television could evoke only lukewarm welcome in India unlike the grandeur with which cinema, the marvel of the century was received in India nearly one hundred years earlier. The then Prime Minister, Pandit Jawaharlal Nehru was even indifferent to open television as he regarded it only as a luxury meant to meet the needs of the middle class. Even the public at large were reluctant to purchase TV sets as television was portrayed as an aid to the development programmes and not a novelty form of entertainment. Systematic application of television for education was initiated with the aid of Ford Foundation since 1961. The TV sets provided for this purpose initially covered 144 schools with the proposal to cover all the schools in Delhi in due course. The scheme was to relay systematic inschool instructional programmes on selected subjects as a supplement to regular school instruction. Under the scheme, programmes in chemistry, physics, English, Hindi and current affairs were initially telecast to the 9th class students. The scheme was extended to the middle school children at a subsequent date. By 1964 about 35,000 students viewed science lessons, 50,000 students current affairs and 25,000 students English lessons.

Television unit also undertook a project on social education with the cooperation of UNESCO Programmes on educational and informative themes and began to broadcast twice a week for a duration of 40 to 70 minutes as part of the scheme. Tele-clubs, numbering more than 180 with a membership of more 3,600 were formed under the scheme by 1964.[2] Programmes to cover themes of interest to women, youth and children were added later. A pilot project for promoting better agricultural practices and to popularize family planning was inaugurated in 1967. Television sets were provided to the tele-clubs by the government. Around this time, a Commission was appointed to study the feasibility of television for education. The Commission, known as Chanda Commission made a few recommendations as the guidelines for the future course of action in utilizing television in India for education and development. The recommendations of the Commission were: (1) a daily school service for all middle and higher secondary schools; (2) in service training for school teachers and village level workers suitably adjusted to the differing needs of each state; (3) a daily programme for agricultural workers, for which all relevant information and guidance would be provided for the rural community on agricultural matters, interspersed with light entertainment to hold the attention of the viewers; (4) a daily social education service which would include literacy lessons, programmes for women, information and entertainment suitable for semi-educated and illiterate adults and (5) programmes for children.[3] The commission was inspired by the ideas of people like Schramm who believed that television can serve the purpose of development by telecasting appropriate programmes. The transmittig station located in Delhi was the only one available in the country till then. New stations were opened at Mumbai, Calcutta, Amristar, Pune, Srinagar, Lucknow and Chennai by 1975. TV facilities began to expand in size since then. Though primary importance was given to educational and instructional programmes, other pogrammes were also added. Those thus included comprised news, feature films, music programmes, television plays, foreign comedies, and a large number of other programmes. With this a change in the content from that of mere development theme to that of entertainment was also on the anvil.

An important development was the formation of National Satellite Communication Group in 1968 at the initiative of Dr. Vikram Sarabhai. In turn, government of India approved a hybrid television broadcasting system consisting of communication satellites as well as ground based microwave relay transmitters. Sarabhai visualized that the satellite component would follow into leap frog with the state of the art of communication technology and would speed up the process of development.[4]

The most important development of this period on the basis of Sarabhai's initiative was the launching of Satellite Instructional Television Experiment (SITE). It was a one year satellite broadcast project to reach millions of rural people in 2,400 villages. Launched in 1975-76, its objectives were to improve rural primary education, provide teacher training, improve agriculture, health and hygiene and to contribute to family planning. The launching of SITE provided sufficient experience in satellite hardware, television software costs and field based operational management issues.[5] SITE could expose the power of television to the entire country and thereby of its impact on every aspect of life.[6] Khedda Communication Project (KCP) was a similar one undertaken for educational purpose.

Under the scheme, one-low power-transmitter connected to a local studio at Pij, a village 50 kms south of Ahemadabad, was connected to the local Doordarshan station and to a satellite earth station in Ahmedabad. Naturally, KCP was equipped to broadcast both local television programmes and national satellite television programmes. Some 650 community television sets provided to 400 villages were installed in public places where village audiences could gather and view the programmes. The project promoted rural development and social change at local level. Participation of audience was vigorously encouraged at all levels. Villagers were involved as actors, writers, and visualisers in the production of television programmes dealing with such local issues of exploitation, caste discrimination, minimum wages, alcoholism, cooperatives and so on. Issues such as family planning, gender equality, village sanitation etc. were also addressed through television serials, puppet shows, folk drama, and other formats. In the words of Singhal "the Khedda project represented a model of community-level decentralised television broadcast in India". It could secure the UNESCO prize for rural communication effectiveness in 1984 and world wide recognition. Unfortunately, "the Indian government did not replicate the KCP community based television model in other parts of India" lamented Singhal.[7]

The Era of Developments

Site was only a beginning in the development of television in various directions. Hitherto, television concentrated on education and development. Practically no attention was given to entertainment. Television was a state monopoly with no private participation or commercial element. A debate was taking place in policy making circles whether entertainment should be given due consideration. It was contended that a poor country like India cannot afford entertainment programmes which call for high cost. Finally, financial considerations tilted the scale in favour of entertainment for which sustenance was sought through commercial advertisements. Accordingly, TV became commercial by introducing advertisements, though on a limited scale from 1 January 1976. Advertisement during this period consisted of slides or cardboard captions for ten second exposure before and at the end of the program.[8] There has however, been practically no sponsorship except portions of cricket matches, a lawn tennis at Calcutta, and a solitary instance of a fashion parade in Delhi and Bombay.[9]

A far more significant development was the introduction of colour TV. Though colour became the standard with most of the countries, Government of India was resisting the introduction of colour TV for economic reasons.[10] At last by 1982, government of India veered around colour TV. It was formally inaugurated with the Independence day speech of the then Prime Minister, Smt. Indira Gandhi on 15 August 1982. The introduction of colour was followed by ASIAD which is termed the Asian Games. The ASIAD was telecast all over the nation in full colour with financial sponsorship from major private corporations. ASIAD was a path breaking event in the history of television in India with which the entire country was transformed as another country. Close on the heels of ASIAD, many policy changes were in the air. One of them was to increase in the number of commercial spots on television. A second development was an increase in entertainment programmes. A third one was the adoption of sponsored programs under which the government sold time to the advertisers to air independently produced television programmes. As Mitra puts, "this quasi-commercialisation saw the advent of a greater number of entertainment programs—from live sports to serialized soap opera".[11] The introduction of a regular satellite link between Delhi and other transmitters facilitating the formation of national network was another important development taken place in 1982.

On the basis of the experience gained from SITE, the Indian national satellite, INSAT–1A was launched by NASA in 1982. Since it developed technical problems, it was deactivated within months. Another satellite-INSAT–1B was launched in 1983. It is reported that over one hundred Indian engineers were at work at Ford Aerospace where it was constructed. Following the success of INSAT other generation satellites were launched leading to the further expansion of television facilities. Under the scheme, production studios could uplink the programmes to INSAT satellites which down linked them to the station transmitters which in turn rebroadcast the programmes to the surrounding area. At the same time, the number of stations which was only one in 1959, increased to five in 1973, 19 in 1983 and to 175 in 1985. Similarly there was expansion in television accessibility in India. In 1983 only 30 million people regularly watched television. By 1988, 62 per cent of the population had access to television and over 100 millions watched television progammes regularly.[12]

Beginnings of Cable

As seen in the previous chapter, cable had emerged in the US for linking television programmes in places where visibility was very poor on account of the obstruction caused by the tall buildings or trees. Developments on similar lines were at work in India also. Cable began to appear during 1980s in Mumbai where multistoried buildings could be connected much more conveniently, by cable from a master antenna, than to connect each households with separate antennas. However, some other peculiar developments were actually instrumental for the emergence of cable in a big way. Though DD had started entertainment programmes from 1970s, its morning transmission began only in 1987 and afternoon programmes two years later. Apparently, the entertainment programmes of DD were neither sufficient in volume, nor at the appropriate time of the day to meet the growing thirst for entertainment. Around this time, VCRs introduced in the country by the expatriate Indians returning from foreign countries became handy for meeting the growing demand for entertainment. People could watch Hindi, Tamil, Malayalam and other language films by connecting the VCRs to television sets. In turn, the VCR system turned out to be the crucial factor to the widespread growth of cable TV throughout India. Bhatt explains the evolution of cable thus: "From watching films on VCRs at home to community viewing with the help of a cable was only a logical step that was taken by some dynamic operators in Bombay in 1984. Instead of a home VCR watching, a small group of activity, the cable TV brought a film or two every day for a monthly payment of around Rs. 150 and a one time payment of Rs. 400 or 500, as a security or installation charges".[13] Houses wired with cable could be connected to a VCR from the control room of the cable operators. Many small entrepreneurs like, Dinyar Contractor, Yogesh Radhakrishnan, Jajit Kohli, Yogesh Shah etc., to name only a few, sensed the possibility of exhibiting movies and other serials through VCR to households connected with cable and making good profit. What they did was to set up a small control room with an antenna and a VCR in the apartment block, and to connect the households in the locality with the cable wire and to relay one or two movies or other entertainment programmes in addition to the regular TV programmes. To the members of the households who were dissatisfied with the sterile programmes of Doordarshan the movies and other entertainment programmes relayed through the VCRs were like a godsent blessing to satisfy their entertainment needs.[14]

The total investment of a small cable operator of such a category came around Rs. 20,000 or so. He charged each household a small monthly fee of about Rs. 75 in addition to the installation charge of about Rs. 500. A cable operator could cover the break even point by connecting at least 150 households. Many of them were able to connect about 750 households and to earn Rs. 50,000 or more. They could thus make huge profit. Since it was illegal to form such video distribution system under the Indian Telegraph Act 1885, police occasionally raided the control rooms of the cable operators. Skirmishes also broke out between the operators, copyright holders and film producers on various occasions. However, cable networks continued to swell rapidly and by 1990 there were about 3,500 cable operators in Mumbai.[15]

It first spread to various parts of Maharastra and Gujarat

in quick succession and then to other places like Delhi. Interestingly, Asianet cable in Kerala was able to make an agreement with the State Electricity Board for the distribution of TV signals to the households by using the poles of the Electricity Board which carry electricity in the state.[16] As an enterprise cable was started without any legal regulation. Eventually, The Cable Television Regulation Act of 1994 brought the cable operators under the purview of legal provisions. Once satellite channels began broadcasting in India, cable operators realized that they could install satellite receiving dishes to catch the signals of those channels like CNN. In fact, as Owen Thomas enjoins, the growth of viewership for all channels through satellite was due to the pre-existence of cable operators in urban areas in India.[17] However, with the entry of more private channels, cable business slipped from the hands of small entrepreneurs and bigger entrepreneurs took over the reins. Larger cable operators or broadcasters started to set up control rooms or overheads with dishes capable of receiving many more channels with which they could offer the signals to small operators who in turn gave the signals to the TV owners. The system is known as Multi System Operators. Thus United Cable Network of Mumbai, Hathway Cables, RPG Cables, Siticable of Zee TV came into existence. With this the number of small operators sharply declined.[18] Big operator acquired the position of a wholesaler while small operators became retailers in the set up. Needless to say, Cable connections continued to swell at a quick pace. It is reported that as many as 42 million households were connected with cable by 2000.[19] The latest reports indicate that cable connections have gone upto 68 million by 2006.[20] Thus the cable system evolved out of the already established system for videos has grown as a gigantic activity within a decade. On the other hand, cable was very slow to penetrate in Great Britain and other European countries. In Great Britain for example, there were only 6,11,000 cable connections which accounted for 3 per cent of the TV households in 1993.[21]

Entry of Private Channels

Broadcasting was a subject reserved for the central government as per Article 246 of the Constitution. With the liberalization policy initiated in 1991, some of the exclusive monopolies of the state were thrown open to the private sector. Such a change in policy could eventually facilitate the entry of private sector in the development of television. However, certain other developments particularly relating to technology have been instrumental in accelerating the process of private participation in broadcasting.

An interesting development was at work in the evolution of private broadcasting in India. Till 1990 the only channel which was allowed to operate in India was Doordarshan. However, around this time satellite channels were beaming programmes all over the world. Signals from channels which can be retransmitted through a satellite can be received in any set with the help of a dish antenna. Some hotels like Taj, Oberoi in the metropolitan cities were already receiving progammes from channels like CNN with the help of dish antenna. When the first Gulf war started in 1991, many citizens of India who had relatives in the Gulf region flocked anxiously to such hotels to see the actual course of war as retransmitted through the dish antennas. Needless to say, it created an urge in the minds of people to see the programmes transmitted by the television channels from other countries and also what was going on in other parts of the world. Sensing the mood of the people, some cable operators began to erect dish antennas and retransmit the programmes from foreign TV channels. In course of time some channels established their own networks of cable or some of them even purchased a number of cable television systems as in the case of Siticable, a cable television network owned by Zee-TV. Thus foreign private channels began to invade the domestic market.

The first private channel which entered in the Indian market by adopting this method was STAR—TV with headquarters at Hong Kong. The word STAR itself stands for Satellite Television for the Asian Region. The channel, was started by Hutch Vision Group of Hong Kong in August 1991 after purchasing ASIASAT 1, a satellite stationary over the Indian ocean. STAR's programmes are targeted at the urban elites in Hong Kong, Taiwan, China, Japan, Indonesia, India and other nations from Japan to Middle East.[22] STAR broadcasts both in Hindi and in English. Executives of STAR are not only conferred with relative freedom to the development of indigenous programmes in India, but also with production techniques, advice and finance. Since 1999, STAR broadcasts in several channels in addition to the five networks with which it originally started Viz; STAR Plus, STAR Sports, Channel V, a music channel, BBC and STAR Mandarin (aimed at Chinese viewers). STAR World which broadcasts English language entertainment programme was started in 1998. In 1995 STAR was purchased by Rupert Murdoch's News Corporation for a price of $871 million. Thus it became an affiliate to a true multinational corporation.

A number of channels followed the example of STAR. Sony corporation of Japan is one of such channels which made an entry in the Indian market in 1995. MTV India is yet another channel which is an offshoot of an Ameican channel which targets the young audience with an endless series of popular music. Discovery channel with head quarters in Maryland in US is yet another channel which began to penetrate Indian market from 1995. Its programmes are basically with educationally oriented contents.

While foreign channels were thus penetrating in India, another curious development facilitated the beginning of private telecasting from Indian soil. As no channel other than Doordarshan was allowed to telecast from Indian soil, enterprising businessmen visualized the possibility of uplinking the programmes to satellite transponders from Hong Kong, Singapore, Moscow or other sites outside India and to delink the same with dish antenna erected in India. By taking advantage of this possibility, private businessmen in India, began to send videos of programmes through couriers to those centres in foreign lands and to get them relayed from there and in turn receive them through antennas in India. Thus they skillfully circumvented the prohibition of private broadcasting from India. In course of time, more and more private channels started to telecast programmes from foreign lands. Subsequently private channels were allowed to telecast directly from India. This development accelerated not only the growth of private channels but also the expansion of cable TV. The Indian owned channel, Zee TV opened in October 1992 was the first native channel to enter in the fray. It was Subash Chandra, an Indian multi-millionaire who opened the channel after making an arrangement with STAR group for sharing the satellite slot. Subsequently he expanded his endeavour by opening specialized channels for music, cinema, education etc. He also launched sub regional channels with the brand name Alpha in Marathi, Gujarati, Punjabi and Bengali.[23] An important development in the south was the opening of Sun TV, a Tamil channel by Dayanidhi Maran in April 1993, with an initial investment of Rs. 2.5 million. Subsequently, it spread its tentacles in other linguistic markets in the south by acquiring controlling stakes in Gemini, a Telugu channel and set up Udaya, a Kannada channel and the Malayalam channel Surya TV.

Taking advantage of the openings made by the satellites, Asianet, a Malayalam channel was opened in 1993 at the initiative of Sasi Kumar. It beams its programmes through the Russian satellite Ekran-M. Unlike the other channels, it pays more attention to news, current affairs and documentaries. Sincce Kerala did not have cable network at that time, Asianet opened 15 satellite dish farms in the state with which signals from various satellites were downlinked and distributed to the households. This cable system was set up as stated earlier, with the support of the State Electricity Board which permitted its poles for connecting the cables. Asinet is credited for pioneering multi-service providers which dominate the Indian satellite and cable television industry like web portal, internet services, interactive games, voice data transmission, and educational, music and other channels.[23] In Andhra Pradesh, the media enterprise of Ramoji Rao, opened Enadu TV in 1995.[24]

Since 1990s, a large number of private channels have sprung

up at the national, and regional levels. Asia Tele Network, a Hindi channel launched in 1992 and Jain channel devoted mainly to marketing information were some of the other important channels launched during the initial stages. More channels were started by taking advantage of the 1998 legislation allowing uplinking from Indian soil. Prominent among them are NDTV, Ag Tuck, Jaya, Raj, Kairali, Jeevan, Indiavision, Manorama Vision and so on. Thus there is a mushroom growth of channels since 1990s. They target their programmes at specialised audiences at the national or regional levels.

An equally important development is the domestication of transnational channels. by suitably adapting their programmes to the domestic conditions. At the same time, domestic channels also venture into the foreign lands by catering to the requirements of the expatriates in various foreign countries. This process of globalizing television and domestication of transnational television have been later day development.[25] All these channels are commercials which operate for making a profit. Advertisement forms the main source of income for them.

Public Broadcasting

As already stated, TV was started as a public broadcasting system under the ownership of government of India. When started, it was only an insignificant wing of the All India Radio. On 1 April 1976, it was separated from the All India Radio, with a new name Doordrshan. Nevertheless, it functioned as another department of the central government. In order to free Doordarshan from government control and interference from the politicians, the Prasar Bharati Act was passed by the parliament in 1990. The Act provides for autonomy to Prasar Bharati Corporation, the agency entrusted to manage the enterprise and envisages certain noble ideals like upholding the unity of the country etc. Though the Act was passed in 1990, it was actually implemented only in 1997. Prasar Bhrati, the public broadcasting corporation of India, created by the

Act comprising All India Radio, and Doordarshan came into existence on 23 November 1997. The major objectives of the Corporation as laid down in the Act are as follows: (1) upholding the unity and integrity of the country and the values enshrined in the constitution; (2) promoting national integration; (3) safeguarding citizens right to be informed on all matters of public interest and presenting a fair and balanced flow of information; (4) paying special attention to the fields of education and spread of literacy, agriculture, rural development, health and family welfare and science and technology; (5) creating awareness about women's issues and taking special steps to protect the interests of children, the aged and other vulnerable sections of the society; (6) providing adequate coverage to diverse cultures sports and games and youth affairs; (7) promoting social justice, safeguarding the rights of the working class, minorities and tribal communities and (8) expanding broadcasting facilities and promoting research and development in broadcast technology. Indeed, the objectives cover everything under the sun. The Corporation is governed by a board comprising a chairman, an executive member, a finance member, six part-time members and one member representing the government. At present, Doordarshan operates four all India channels, 11 regional language satellite channels, 8 Hindi belt kendras, one international channel and two parliament channels. Except the Hindi belt channels, all the other channels broadcast round the corner.

Channel DD 1 (National) of Doordarshan is the largest terrestrial network in the world. Nearly 90.7 per cent of the population of the country comes within the coverage of this channel. Being a public broadcasting channel, it makes significant contributions to accelerate socio-economic changes, promote national integration, stimulate scientific temperament, disseminate knowledge, educate the masses on the means of population control, spread the messages of family welfare, preservation of environmental and ecological balance. It also promotes sports, and cultural heritage of the country. Entertainment programmes including serials, films etc. are being telecast. All national events like Republic Day parade, Independence Day celebrations, President's address to the nation, parliamentary debates are being covered live in DD National.

Regional Language Satellite Service, consists of: (1) DD—Malayalam, (2) DD—Bengali, (3), DD—Oriya, (4) DD—Gujarati, (5) DD—Punjabi, (6) DD—Podhigai (Tamil), (7) DD—Saptagiri (Telugu), (8) DD—Chandani (Kannada), (9)DD—Sahyadri (Marathi), (10) DD—North-East and (11) DD—Kashir. These channels broadcast a wide spectrum of programmes encompassing development news, serials, documentaries news and current affairs in the respective local language. The Regional State Networks cater to the people living in Hindi belt comprising UP, Bihar, Jharkhand, Chattisgarh, MP, Rajasthan, Haryana and Himachal Pradesh.

DD News was launched on 3 November 2003 by converting the then existing DD Metro into a 24 hour channel. This is the only terrestrial-cum-satellite, bilingual news channel in the country. News bulletins, news updates, breaking news are scrolled continuously during the transmission. A network of 22 regional news units spread across the country support DD News apart from putting out regional language bulletins.[26] It also covers commercial and promotional packaging or cross-channel publicity. News on stocks and commodities are being relayed throughout the day.

Started in march 1999, DD Sports serves as the country's only free to air sports channel. All cricket matches organized by the Board of Control of Cricket in India, and sports in India like football, hockey, tennis, badminton are telecast by DD Sports. Sports events organized by the different sports federations and associations are also covered by this channel. A cash out flow system was introduced to cover non-olympic and traditional sports.

Lunched on 26 January 2002, DD Bharati telecasts programmes on health, children, music, dance and heritage. Programmes on adventure, quiz contests, fine arts, cartoon, crafts ad presentations are also covered. It telecasts programmes received from Public Service Broadcasting Service and UNESCO. Progrmmes on theatre, literature, music, painting, sculpture, architecture etc., also find space in the shows of this channel's programmes. In collaboration with organizations like IGNOU, CEC, PSBT, NCERT, DD Bharati telecasts educational programmes also. Thus it serves mostly for telecasting programmes with a cultural or educational orientation.

In order to give international coverage to social, cultural, political and economic issues, DD India was launched on March 1995. The objective of the channel is to retain lines of communication with Indians living abroad and to show the real India, its values, culture, its modernity, its diversity, agony and ecstasy to the entire world. The channel carries live news bulletins, features on topical events, entertainment programmes, feature films etc. Programmes from regional languages like Urudu, Marathi, Malayalam, Tamil, Telugu, Kannada, Punjabi etc. apart from Hindi and English form the basic characteristic of DD International. Live coverage of national events like Independence Day, Republic Day celebrations, and other happenings of national and international events are regularly relayed through the channel.[27]

When started, TV was a purely public broadcasting system devoted totally to the development of the country. Gradually entertainment programmes were added as a supplement to the main programmes. Of late, entertainment programmes have gained the upper hand, though culture, art, values, heritage etc. still find a place in the programmes. Weightage given to development has more or less disappeared. With the establishment of Prasar Bharati Corporation, it is supposed to have become an autonomous institution. How deep is the autonomy, is a question for which an answer is yet to be found. National, regional and even local level demands have to be catered by Doordarshan. Conflicts between the needs of local requirements and national priorities are likely to erupt.

Distribution of the Channels

There has been a spurt in the number of channels operating in India during recent years. From that of a single channel operating in 1980s the number went upto 261 by the beginning of 2009 in addition to as many as 30 foreign channels beaming regularly in India. A number of channels is also in the offing. The channels can be divided on the basis of language in which the programmes are telecast. Channels in almost all the national languages are in the field. Among them Hindi which is spoken by 42 per cent of the population dominates with a tally of 89 channels. The other linguistic channels in the descending order are: Telugu 26 channels, Tamil 25 channels, Malayalam 18 channels, Kannada and Bengali 15 each, Punjabi and Marathi 11 each, Oriya 6 and so on. In addition, as many as 33 channels broadcast programmes in English.[28] Though the number of channels exceeds 261, the corporate bodies or concerns which own the channels may not be so much. as most of such concerns own more than one channel.

Channels can also be divided on the basis of the thematic contents of the programmes telecast. They are thus broadly divided as entertaintment, news and sports channels. There are also channels which specialize in children's programmes and religious programmes. Channels like DD1 which telecast entertainment, news, religious and sport programmes fall within the category of mixed category. During the formative days of TV, all channels belonged to the mixed group broadcasting all those kinds of programmes. It was only with the proliferation of channels, specialized channels began to appear. Entertainment channels with a tally of 134 topped the list followed by news channels with 59 and sports with 25 channels respectively.[29]

Competition Among the Channels

Till the entry of private channels during 1990s, Doordarshan had the monopoly in terms of reach and viewership among the audience. With the entry of private channels, Doordarshan lost much of its territory. Even then, Doordarshan continues to be the most important channel in the country. In 1998 DD1 alone claimed a total number 331 million home viewers apart from the viewership of its affiliates like DD2 and the regional channels.[30] All the private channels put together could command only an audience strength of 81.5 million even in

2002. None of the channels could come any where near DD1, even in 2002. Some of the regional channels of DD had bigger share of audience. Among the private channels Star Plus topped the list, followed by Sony and Zee TV. Table 4.1 gives the size of viewership among the different private channels.

Table 4.1: Reach and Viewership of Private Channels in India in 2002

Name of the Channel	Reach			Viewership			Viewership as Ratio to Reach
	Urban	Rural	Total	Urban	Rural	Total	
ESPN	35.01	3.0	19.9	4.7	0.2	2.2	11.05
ETC	19.0	3.2	11.5	1.4	0.4	0.8	6.95
Fashion TV	17.7	0.5	9.5	0.5	—	0.2	0.02
Gemini TV	18.1	9.4	14.0	8.3	6.6	7.3	52.14
HBO	23.8	0.8	12.9	2.1	—	0.9	6.97
Jaya TV	12.1	7.0	9.7	4.1	2.4	3.2	32.98
SABe TV	18.0	0.5	9.7	1.5	0.1	0.7	7.21
Sahara TV	27.4	8.1	18.3	2.3	2.2	2.2	12.02
Set Max	29.8	2.3	16.8	4.5	0.3	2.1	12.50
Sony TV	46.1	12.9	30.4	22.9	5.0	12.8	42.10
Star Gold	25.2	0.9	13.7	1.8	0.1	0.8	5.83
Star movies	40.4	4.1	23.2	4.4	0.3	2.1	9.05
Star News	35.7	2.0	19.7	3.6	0.1	1.6	8.12
Star Plus	52.1	6.3	30.4	28.4	1.5	13.1	43.09
Star Sports	45.2	6.1	26.7	7.5	0.7	3.7	13.83
Star World	24.4	0.9	13.2	0.8	0.1	0.4	3.03
Sun News	15.7	2.0	9.2	1.9	0.3	0.1	1.08
Sun/sun Music	21.8	11.3	16.8	10.0	6.7	8.1	48.21
Surya TV	13.7	3.0	8.6	2.0	1.3	1.6	18.60
Teja TV	9.9	5.7	7.9	3.0	1.9	2.4	30.37
Udya TV	12.8	5.2	9.2	4.5	4.5	4.5	48.91
Vijaya TV/Star Vijay	10.9	7.5	9.3	4.8	2.8	3.7	39.78
Zee Cinema	40.4	4.0	23.1	13.1	1.1	6.3	27.27
Zee News	31.7	2.6	17.9	5.6	0.3	2.6	14.52
Zee TV	47.06	13.7	31.5	19.8	5.5	11.7	37.15
Base 000s	42,911	38,668	81,579	42,911	38,668	81,579	

Note: Viewership: per cent who actually watch in an average week.
Source: *Doordrshan India 2003,* Prasar Bharati Broadcasting Corporation of India.

As can be seen from the Table, viewership was much lower than that of the reach of the channels in al the cases. However, the total number of viewers of all the channels taken together was more than 100 per cent in the urban areas. Apparently, some of the people viewed the programmes of more than one channel. On the other hand, only 43 per cent of the people in the rural areas covered by the channels viewed the programmes. It follows that all the satellite channels listed in the Table have not become very popular with the rural audience. Moreove, cable has not penetrated deeply in all parts of the rural areas of the country.

As the Table indicates viewership was the largest with Star Plus followed by Sony TV, Zee TV, Sun TV/Sun Music, Gemini TV, Zee Cinema etc. in the descending order. On the other hand, the ratio of viewership to the coverage of channels was the highest with Gemini, followed by Sun Music, Sony, Zee TV etc. in the descending order. Apparently, these channels are endowed with higher competitive strength in attracting more number of audience. Percentage of viewership was very low in respect of other channels. However, Star TV, Zee TV and Sun have also their affiliates. If the viewerships of the affiliates are also added with the main channel, Star will be accounting for 21.7 per cent of the viewership, Zee 20.6 per cent and Surya Group 9.8 per cent respectively. However if the quantum of receipts from advertisement is taken as the criterion, Zee would top the list followed by Sony, Star and Surya in the descending order. Zee's strength stems mainly because it caters to the wider Hindi market with appropriate Hindi programmes.[31]

Penetration of TV

Expansion of channels by itself cannot ensure the growth of TV. What is aired through the channels is meant to be seen by the people. They can do this, if enough facilities to watch them are available. There should, therefore be enough receiving sets in the country. In other words, the penetration of TV is dependent on a widespread distribution of receiving sets.

Since TV was started as an experimental measure, receiving sets were only very few in numbers during the initial stages. Interestingly, there were only 21 TV receivers in 1959 when the first broadcasting took place in Delhi. On the other hand, as many as four hundred television sets were sold at the time of the actual opening of television in Great Britain on

2nd November, 1936.[32] The number began to rise only with the expansion of broadcasting facilities in the other metropolitan cities. Even then, there were not many sets. As a matter of fact, it was the people who had been to foreign countries were those who possessed TV sets during the initial stages. The number which was only 28,000 in 1970 increased to 3 million by 1980. The real expansion took place with the entry of commercial channels and the proliferation of broadcasting facilities. By 1997 it went upto 63,000,000 and it is stated to have gone up to 79,374,000 in 2001.[33] There was thus an expansion of TV facilities by more than 300 times within a span of 30 years. In no other country there has been such an unprecedented rate of growth of television facilities. In terms of number of television sets, India became the fourth ranking country in the world. US, Japan and China are the only countries with more number of television receivers. On the other hand in 1970, all the countries with the exception of Bangladesh and Kenya were having more number of TV sets than that of India. (See Table 4.2)

Table 4.2: Availability of TV Receivers in Various Countries Since 1970

Name of the Country	*1970*	*1980*	*1990*	*1997*
India	28 (0.1)	3,000 (4.4)	27,000 ((32)	63,000 (85)
Pakistan	99 (1.5)	938 (11)	1,489 (17)	3,100 (22)
Bangladesh	8 (0.1)	80 (0.9)	525 (4.8)	770 (6.3)
Malaysia	130 (1.2)	1,200 (87)	2,640 (149)	3,600 (172)
Indonesia	90 (0.7)	3,000 (28)	10,500 (57)	13,750 (68)
Thailand	250 (7)	1,000 (21)	5,900 (106)	15,190 (254)
China	660 (0.6)	9,020 (9)	3,09,001 (267)	4,00,000 (321)
Japan	35,000 (335)	62,976 (539)	75,500 (611)	86,500 (686)
Australia	2,758 (220)	5,600 (384)	8,200 (487)	10,150 (554)
Canada	7,100 (333)	10,617 (432)	17,019 (612)	21,500 (710)
USA	84,600 (403)	1,55,800 (676)	2,03,000 (799)	2,19,000 (806)
Mexico	1,800 (36)	3,820 (57)	12,350 (148)	25,600 (272)
Brazil	6,100 (64)	15,000 (123)	30,800 (208)	36,500 (223)
United Kingdom	18,000 (324)	20,200 (359)	24,425 (433)	30,500 (521)
France	12,000 (236)	15,000 (285)	22,800 (402)	34,800 (595)
Germany			44,000 (554)	46,500 (567)
Russian Federation			53,978 (364)	60,500 (410)
Egypt	529 (15)	1,400 (32)	5,700 (108)	7,700 (119)
Kenya	16 (1.4)	62 (3.7)	225 (9.6)	730 (26)

Source: *UNESCO Yearbook*, 1999.[34]

Note: Figures in the bracket indicate TV receivers per 1,000 persons.

Note 2; The number of TV households in India increased to 112 million by 2006; see *The Hindu*, 30th August, 2007.[35] The number seems to have gone upto 130 milion households by 2008 (see Foot Note 20).

However, the volume of TV receivers by itself cannot indicate the extent of penetration of TV in a country. Instead, the ratio of TV sets to the population can be a better criterion. In 1970 there were only 0.1, TV receivers for every 1,000 people in India. It increased to 4.4 in 1980 and to 32 in 1990. It has however, come upto 85 by 1997. Apparently, such a sudden increase indicates, a quicker pace of penetration of TV since 1990. However, the ratio has been higher than that of India in all the countries of Europe, America, and many countries of Asia like China, Japan, Malaysia and Thailand. Furthermore, if we take the average size of a family as five members, only 40 per cent of the households possess a television set in India. On the other hand, with 806 television sets for every 1,000 people, a family may be owning on an average about four television sets in the US. Similarly, most of the counties of Europe and China and Japan in Asia also possess more than two television receivers per family. Pakistan, Bangladesh, Indonesia, Kenya and Egypt are the only countries in the list with less than one television set each per household as in the case of India. Similarly, the vast majority of the countries in Asia and Africa may not be possessing one television receivers each per family.

Distribution of TV Receivers in Various Parts of India

Though TV has penetrated in a big way since 1990s it is not uniformly distributed throughout the country. TV sets are concentrated mainly in the urban areas and the rural areas left out with very few sets. (see Table 4.3)

In actual terms, against 76 per cent of the households in urban areas possessing television sets, only 28 percent of the households in rural areas possess television sets. Apparently, television remains as an urban phenomenon. With 89 percent of the households possessing at least one receiver, Delhi tops

Table 4.3: Statewise Distribution of TV Receivers in India as on 2001 (Figures in thousands)

Name of the State	*Urban*	*Rural*	*Total*
Delhi	2,270 (89.3)	303 (88.3)	2,573 (89.2)
Punjab/Haryana/ Chandigarh/Himachal Pradesh	2,444 (88.6)	4,023 (63.6)	6,467 (71.2)
Rajasthan	1,718 (76.7)	1,765 (25.7)	3,483 (38.2)
Uttar Pradesh	3,703 (68.4)	4,572 (22.2)	8,275 (31.8)
Bihar	1,305 (58.8)	1,481 (10.1)	2,786 (16.5)
N.E. and Assam	1,042 (80)	1,028 (25.3)	2,070 (38.5)
West Bengal	3,173 (69.5)	2,552 (22.3)	5,725 (35.7)
Orissa	734 (69.1)	1,016 (16.6)	1,750 (24.4)
Madhya Pradesh	2,850 (78.3)	2,775 (25.1)	5,625 (38.3)
Gujarat	2,841 (74.6)	1,450 (25.5)	4,291 (45.2)
Maharashtra and Goa	7,460 (82.3)	4,183 (37)	11,643 (57.2)
Karnataka	2,757 (78.8)	2,243 (32.8)	5,000 (48.4)
Kerala	1,219 (67.5)	2,062 (41)	3,281 (48)
Andhra Pradesh	3,894 (74.1)	4,451 (35.5)	8,345 (46.9)
Tamil Nadu & Pondicherry	4,050 (76.4)	4,008 (39.3)	8,058 (51.9)

Source: *Doordarshan India* 2002[36]
Note: Figures in the bracket indicate percentage of households with TV sets.

the list. This high percentage is due mainly to the urban character of Delhi. While 71 per cent of the households in Punjab, Haryana, Himachal Pradesh and Chattisgarh owned television receivers, Bihar occupies the lowest bottom with hardly 17 per cent of the households owning television sets. The southern states like Kerala, Karnataka, Tamil Nadu and Andhra Pradesh veer around the all India average. On the other hand, most of the Hindi speaking states are far below the national average. Apparently, a large number of people of the country especially of the rural areas do not have the facility to watch television programmes. Thus the penetration of TV is somewhat uneven in the country in spite of the growth of TV.

Economic Significance of Television Industry

As already mentioned in Chapter 2, television forms a branch of the culture industry which carries on productive activities on factory lines. Ipsofacto, economic parameters like capital investment, output, volume of employment etc. become crucial in the production of the contents of television and the ways in which they are communicated. Television receivers and accessories which form the hard-ware of the industry, carry out the conveyance of the products of television. The production of television receivers have become prominent with the growth of television in all the countries.

Manufacturing of television (hard ware) had a humble beginning in India as in the case of its software component. It was not at all classified as a separate manufacturing activity in the reports of the Annual Survey of Industries published every year by the Central Statistical Organization till 1970. It was clubbed with the industrial sub-group comprising manufacturing of X-ray equipments, tele-printer and other electrical equipments and appliances. The country was able to produce only 5,011, TV sets valuing Rs. 78,55,000 in 1970. Production of television sets was recognised as a separate industrial activity by CSO only since 1971.[37] At that time, there were only two factories engaged in the production of TV sets with a capital investment of Rs. 22.4 million. With the extension of broadcasting facilities to Mumbai in 1972, production of TV receivers seems to have received a boosting. Since then, it began to grow at a fast rate in terms of capital investment, output and all other parameters related to the production of television sets in our country. Table 4.4 gives the volume of output, capital investment and other details relating to the production of television receivers during recent years starting with the year 1973-74.

Since the industry was in its infancy the volume of capital investment, the output, the number of persons employed etc. were all meagre in magnitude in 1973-74. The introduction of colour in the beginning of 1980s would have promoted the growth of the industry only on a limited scale. However, the entry of private channels in 1990s seems to have been the turning point in its growth. As can be seen from the Table, the growth rate of various facets of the industry has been phenomenal since 1973-74. By 2002-03 the number of factories went up to 251 from a meagre size of 10 in 1973-74. The volume of invested capital increased to Rs. 56,504 million in 2002-03

Table 4.4: Profile of Television (hardware) Industry in India Over the Years

(amount rupees in million)

Sl. No.	*Name of the Parameter*	*1973-74*	*1983-84*	*1993-94*	*2002-03*
1.	Number of factories	10	81	203	253 (25.30)
2.	Fixed capital	10.25	151.17	17,139.37	34,397.9 (3,355)
3.	Invested capital	37.84	596.01	2,1035.0	56,504.5 (1,493)
4.	Value of output	46.86	2,066.58	29,783.18	1,68,968.7 (3,605)
5.	Net value added	4.37	244.10	4,254.46	17,778.6 (4,068)
6.	No. of persons engaged	1,506	7,383	28,754	29,291 (19.44)
7	No. of television sets produced (B&W)	20,279	1,04,553	38,74,131	11,98,233 (59)
8.	Value (Rs.)	35.31	1,238.77	10,197.0	2,675.69
9.	Television sets (colour)	—	2,63,694	8,37,367	61,41,772
10.	Value (Rs.)		3,602.28	8,220.68	45,564.91

Source: CSO; *Annual Survey of Industries* various years.[38]
Note: Figures in the bracket indicate the ratio of various parameters of television industry in 2002-03 to those in 1973-04.

from a sum of Rs. 37.84 million in 1973-2004 recording a growth of more than 1,493 times within a period of less than thirty years. The volume of output and net value added stood at Rs. 1,68,968 and Rs. 17,778.6 million respectively in 2002-03. While the increase in value of the output was more than 3,605 times over its level in 1973-74, the increase in the case of net value added was more than 4,068 times. As a source of employment television manufacturing industry could provide employment to 29,293 persons in 2002-03. As can be seen from the Table with the production of 61,41,772 colour television sets, in 2002-03 the country has emerged as a major producer of television sets.

The unprecedented growth of television industry has resulted in its emergence as an important segment of the industrial sector in India during recent years. Table 4.5 gives the percentage share of television industry to the factory sector of India.

Since its beginnings in 1970s production of television has grown as an important unit of the factory sector in India. No other industrial sector has achieved such a phenomenal rate of growth within a short period of its beginning. Though its share of capital investment or net value added as a percentage

Table 4.5: Ratio of Television Industry to the Factory Sector of India as on 2004-05

Sl. No.	*Name of Parameter*	*All India Totals*	*Television Industry*
1.	No. of factories	1,36,353	271 (0.19)
2.	Fixed Capital (Rs. million)	51,30,692.5	53,317 (1.03)
3.	Invested Capital (Rs. million)	75,94,177.0	82,780.8 (1.09
4.	Value of Output (...)	1,67,25,614.2	1,95,452.7 (1.16)
5.	Net Value Added (...)	25,99,068.6	12,846.0 (0.49)
6.	No. of Persons Employed	84,53,624	29,676 (0.35)

Source: CSO; *Annual Survey of Industries 2004-2005,* New Delhi, 39.

to all India total revolves around one per cent, it occupies an important place among the hundreds of industrial sectors in India. In fact, in respect of these aspects, it is bigger in size compared to many other industrial activities in India.

Contribution to the Economy in Terms of Employment and Output

As in the case of the hardware sector of the industry, the software side also contributes in a big way in generating income and employment in the country. However, there are many theoretical and practical difficulties for measuring the income generated by television. Since it is a service activity, determination of output, let alone valuation of output baffles measurement. In services like transport, the passenger mile is reckoned as the yardstick for measuring the output. Occupancy rate is the usual method adopted in hoteliering. In film industry the visit turn over is very often adopted as the norm. None of these criteria can be applicable in the case of television for various reasons. First, anybody with an antenna can get the signal and see the programme. The usual method to overcome this difficulty is to levy a license fee from all the TV owners. In UK license fee is the main source of revenue to BBC. Since license fee has been abolished in India from 1984, it cannot be used to measure the volume of output. Second, any programme becomes a source of income only if it is utilised by the consumer. There are more than two hundred and odd television channels which broadcast programmes throughout the day.

Such programmes become output in the economic sense, only if they are seen by the audience. Otherwise they remain as a free good with no economic value. The audience decides as to which programme is to be selected.

However, as we have seen, cable TV has become an important means of conveyance of programmes to the TV owners. In the absence of any other viable yardstick the fees levied by cables can be reckoned as one yardstick for measuring the income generated by the TV. Any subscriber of cable pays on an average a monthly fee of Rs. 200 to the cable operator. There were about 38 million cable connections in our country in 2001. At the rate of Rs. 2,400 per subscriber per year, the revenue generated would have been around Rs. 80,000 million in 2001. Interestingly, cable began to appear in India only from 1990s. The number of cable connections was stated to be 1.2 million in 1992. According to an author it would have fetched a revenue of Rs. 1008 million in 1992.[40] Apparently the earnings have increased by about 80 times within a period of 10 years. However, not all households are owners of cable TV. There were 79 million households owning television sets. Apparently, 41 million households are not connected with cable. They also utilize TV programmes. With the abolition of license fee for TV sets in our country, the TV owners for practical purposes get the programmes free of cost. Broadcasters cannot carry on with their programmes without recouping their cost. It is the advertisers who cover the cost of broadcasting by entering in the scene on which further reference will be made in another Chapter. What they pay as advertisement charges or sponsorship fees becomes the revenue to the producers. The total earnings from advertisement came to Rs. 50,240 million in 2001. On the other hand, the total earnings from advertisement was stated to be only Rs. 2,540 million in 1990. Revenue from advertisements increasd by more than twenty times during this period. As a percentage to the total advertisement revenue of all the media, TV could account for 17.7 per cent in 1990. By 2001 its share has gone upto 40.9 per cent.[41] The total amount spent on advertisement and cable which can for practical purposes, be reckoned as the value of the gross product turned out by TV, would thus accounted for Rs. 1,30,240 million 2001. On a per capita basis it works out to more than Rs. 100 per year.

The Gross National Product of the country was estimated at Rs. 2,09,09,570 million in 2001-2.[42] The value of the gross product turnrd out by television would be about 0.62 per cent of the Gross National Product. In addition income is also created by the hardware sector of television industry. As mentioned earlier, the net value added by this sector was Rs. 17,778.6 million in 2002-3. Broadcasting materials are also turned out by the manufacturing sector. The net value added by this sector was Rs. 7,701.5 million in 2002-3.[43] In addition to this, channels also receive various other kinds of revenue like the sale proceeds of slots for local advertisements. In 2006 Jeevan TV for example, received Rs. 14.8 million from the sale of slots against an earnings of Rs. 32.18 from advertisement.[44] It formed 30 per cent of the earnings from advertisements. Other channels would also be receiving earnings like this. Apparently, the gross product rendered by television in our country would be more than 0.62 per cent of the GNP.

Significantly, the importance of television is reflected with the inclusion of the income generated by television as part of the National Product from the 1993-94 series of National Accounting. On the other hand, the income generated by television did not figure at all in the National Accounts of the earlier series as television was contributing only an insignificant proportion of state National Product prior to 1990s.[45] (see also appendix 1). Nevertheless, in the 1993-94 series, the net product of TV is clubbed with other services and no separate figures are given.

Television provides not only income but also employment opportunities on an increasing scale. As seen earlier, the hardware sector was a source of employment for 29,291 persons in 2002-3. Manufacturing activities of broadcasting materials could provide employment to 26,096 persons n 2002-3. The number of persons employed in the Prasar Bharati Corporation was 21,783 in 2002.[46] In addition the various private channels and cable companies provide employment to a large number of persons. It is reported that the cable sector alone was able to provide employment to more than one million people even in 1990s.[47]

In sum, television has grown as a major economic activity in our country within a period of less than fifty years of its arrival. The income generated and employment opportunities created are on the increase every year. It ranks as a major industry in terms of the volume of capital invested as well as in creating income and providing employment. It is poised to grow at a fast rate in the years to come, though the picture is stated to be not so bright in the West.

NOTES AND REFERENCES

1. GOI (Government of India), *India 1960,* New Delhi, Ministry of Information and Broadcasting.
2 GOI. *India 1964,* New Delhi, Ministry of Information and Broadcasting.
3. Mitra, Anand (1993). *Television in India,* New Delhi, Sage Publications, p. 27.
4. Singhal, Aravind, Rogers, Everett M. (2001). *India's Communication Revolution,* New Delhi, Sage Publications, p. 82.
5. Singhal, Arvind and Rogers, Everett M. (2001). *op. cit.,* p. 85.
6. Mitra, Anand (1993). *op. cit.,* p. 34.
7. Singhal, Aravind ar d Rogers, Everett M. (2001). *op. cit.,* p. 96.
8. Mitra, Anand (1993). *op. cit.,* p. 35.
9 GOI (1978). *Report of the Working Group on the Autonomy for Akashvani and Doordarshan Vol. 11,* New Delhi, Ministry of Information and Broadcasting.
10. Mitra, Anand (1993). *op. cit.,* p. 36.
11. Mitra, Anand (1993). *op. cit.,* p. 37.
12. Singhal, Arvind and Rogers, Everett (2001). *op. cit.,* p. 85.
13. Bhatt, S.C. (1994). *Satellite Invasion of India,* New Delhi, Gyan Publishing House, p. 45.
14. Kohli, Anitha (2003). *The Indian Media Business,* New Delhi, Sage, p. 66.
15. Kohli, Anitha (2003). *op. cit.,* p. 67.
16. David, Page and William, Crawley (2001). *Satellites over South Asia: Broadcasting Culture and the Public Interest,* London, Sage, p. 92.
17. Thomas Amos Owen (2005). *Imagi-Nations and Borderless Television,* New Delhi, Sage Publications, p. 128.

18. Kohli, Anitha (2003). *op. cit.*, p. 72.
19. Kohli, Anitha (2003). *op. cit.*, p. 61.
20. According to the National Readership Survey as reported in *The Hindu* the number of homes with cable and satellite television has grown from 61 million in 2005 to 68 million in 2006. see *The Hindu* dated August 30, 2006. The number of homes with TV is reported to have gone upto 130 million and with cable TV, 71 million by 2009.
21. Bob, Mullan (1997). *Consuming Television*, Oxford, Blackwell Publishers, p. 33.
22. Singhal, Aravind and Rogers, Everett M. (2001). *op. cit.*, p. 108.
23. Kohli, Anitha (2003). *op. cit.*, p. 70.
24. Thomas Amos Own (2005). *op. cit.*, New Delhi, Sage, p. 116.
25. David, Page and Crawley, William (2001). *Satellites Over South Asia Broadcasting Culture and the Public Interest*, Sage London, pp. 78-81.
26. GOI; *India 2006*. p. 637.
27. GOI. *Annual Report 2005-06*, New Delhi, Ministry of information and Broadcasting.
28. wikipedia.org. List of Indian Television Stations.
29. wikipedia. *op. cit.*
30. Page and Crawley (2001). *op. cit.*, p. 125.
31. Singhal, Arvind and Rogers, Everett (2001). *op. cit.*, p. 113.
32. Bob, Mullan (1997). *Consuming Television*, Oxford, Blackwell Publishers, p. 21.
33. GOI. *Doordarshan India*, 2002.
34. UNESCO *Yearbook 1999*.
35. *The Hindu*, 30th August, 2006.
36. GOI. *DoordarshanIndia* 2002.
37. GOI. *Annual Survey of Industries 1971-72*, New Delhi, Central Statistical Organisation.
38. GOI. *Annual Survey of Industries various years*, New Delhi, CSO.
39. GOI (2004-05). *Annual Survey of Industries 2004-05*, New Delhi, Central Statistical Organisation.
40. Kohli, Anitha (2003). *op. cit.*, p. 61.
41. Rajya Sabha: *Untarred Question No. 1348* dated 03-12-2001.
42. GOI. *National Accounts* 2002-2003, New Delhi, CSO.
43. GOI. *Annual Survey of Industries 2002*, New Delhi, CSO.
44. Jeevan TV. *Annual Statement of Accounts 2006*, Cochin, 2006.
45. GOI. *National Accounts 2001-02*, New Delhi, CSO.
46. GOI. *Doordarshan India 2003*.
47. Bhatt, S.C. (1994). *op. cit.*, p. 49.

Appendix 1
Capital Investment in the Industry

Industrial activity of any category calls for fairly large volume of capital investment. Television industry cannot be an exception to this general pattern. As already stated in Chapter 4, a fairly large volume of capital amounting to Rs. 56,504 million is invested in the hardware sector of television industry in 2002-03.

In addition to the hardware sector, broadcasting sector, software sector, cable sector and receiving sector constitute the other components of television industry. The fixed capital investment in Doordarshan as on 2004 was stated to be Rs. 55,162.8 million.[1] That leaves the private sector numbering more than 260 in the field. Some of them like STAR, Sony, MTV etc., are foreign channels. Many of the Indian channels like Zee, Sun, Enadu, Asianet and so on, own a network of channels as their affiliates. Incorporated channels in India with their affiliates would be around 100. According to Sardesai, the capital investment in a channel would be between Rs. 500-750 million.[2] At an average investment of Rs. 500 million per channel, the total investment in the incorporated channels can very well be Rs. 50,000 million. Apparently, the investment in the broadcasting sector would be around Rs.1,00,000 million. Interestingly, the volume of marketised capital of some ten channels like Zee, Sun, NDTV, etc. which have listed their shares in the stock market totalled Rs. 39,953 million in 2007-08.[3] Needless to say, it reflects the growing appreciation of the assets of these concerns.

Software sector is perhaps the most important component of the industry. Software sector is concerned with the production of texts which can generate income for a number of years. The ongoing process of production calls for capital for meeting the cost of various inputs. Once produced, they are taken by the channels for transmission. Thus the volume of the capital invested at any time consists of: (a) the amount invested during the ongoing process of production and (b) the amount already invested in the texts in circulation. However, an attempt to measure the volume of capital investment is beset with a number of problems on account of the methodological and operational difficulties. By themselves, the texts are cultural products which defy standardization. At the same time, producers are not in the habit of keeping the accounts. Nor, are they willing to give the proper accounts of the cost of production. Apprently, any attempt to estimate the volume of investment invariably becomes a mere guess work. Oommen and Joseph have made an attempt to estimate the volume of capital investment in film industry by dividing it into (a) the investment made during gestation period in the case of ongoing process of production and (b) the amount invested in the case of films in distribution.[4] Such a method may not be suitable in the case of television as the serials, the important cultural product of television, are made up of episodes meant to be transmitted for each day, are not produced as a completed product but in a piecemeal form as and when they are required to be telecast. At the same time, practically the entire cost of an episode is recouped with the transmission on each day. Nevertheless, as a prudent business practice, a few episodes are produced in one stretch of time and kept in store and as transmission continues, another bunch of episodes is produced. A rough idea on the quantum of capital investment can be formed on the basis of cost of production of a bunch of episodes meant to be transmitted at least for two months. Each channel on an average transmits five episodes a day. At the rate of five episodes per day, the 200 and odd channels in the country would be transmitting 1,000 episodes on any day. The total number would be 3,65,000 episodes in an year. An episode will be costing between Rs. 1,00,000-3,00,000 according to industrial sources. A lower amount would be applicable in the case of the majority of episodes as most of the channels are concerned with regional markets. Moreover, some of the episodes would be reruns. Under such circumstances, if we take Rs. 1,50,000 as the average cost per episode, it would not be wide off the mark. Assuming that they would be relayed within a period of two months of production, the volume of capital invested at a period of time would be around Rs. 9,145 million for the serials made up of numerous episodes. In addition, channels produce other programmes and transmit feature films also.

Conveyance sector consisting of the cable connections constitutes another important segment of the industry. Capital investment is needed for connecting the households and to install costly equipments like the dish antenna. No authentic data on the investment in this sector is available. However, the cable companies collect an installation charge ranging from Rs. 1,000 to 2,000 per household. There were well over 42 million households having cable connection around 2,000. If we assume the installation of Rs. 1,000 as the approximate investment cost per household the total investment in the conveyance sector would be around Rs. 40,000 million.

The receiving component of the industry forms the other sector in which also a large volume of capital is invested. As stated in Chapter 4, there were about 79.37 million television receivers in the country in 2001. All of them might not have been new sets. Actualy there were 27 million sets in 1990. Apparently, 52.37 million sets were added during the 12 year period from 1990-2001 with an addition of 4.36 million sets on an average per year. The ex-factory price of a TV set was estimated at around Rs. 9,817 in 1993-94.[5] If we take the value of a set as Rs. 9,800 in 2002, the value of a set purchased during the earlier periods would be much lower on account of depreciation. Similarly, if we assume depreciation to spread over in a descending order, for the 12 year period from 1990 to 2002 with 100 per cent for the sets purchased in 1990 and earlier, and nil in 2002-03, the total value of the 52.37 million sets would be Rs. 2,34,990 million.

The total of all these items amounts to Rs. 384,135 million which can approximately be regarded as the capital investment in the industry at the beginning of the third millennium. Capial investment of such a magnitude is pretty large according to the Indian standards. In addition the volume of investment in the hardware sector is also fairly big.

REFERENCES

1. GOI. *Prasar Bharati: Annual Report 2005-06* (New Delhi, Broadcastig Corporation of India).
2. Rajdeep Sardesai (2006). "Pushing the Boundaries" in *Seminar* May 2006.
3. Centre for Monitoring Indian Economy (CMIE) (2009). *Capital Markets,* May 2009.
4. Oommen, M.A. and Josph, K.V. (1991). *Economics of Indian Cinema,* New Delhi, Oxford and IBH Publishing Co., p. 58.
5. Central Statistical Organisation (1993-94). *Annual Survey of Industries, 1993-34: Factory Sector.*

5

Programmes

The Product Mix of Television Industry

In the previous chapter, we have delineated the growth and economic significance of Television in India. TV as already mentioned in the Introduction, constitutes an important branch of culture industry. As an activity, culture industry engages in the production and transmission of texts in which creative contents with signs and symbols are embodied in them. Such texts are turned out on regular factory lines with the aid of advanced technological instruments. Economic parameters like large scale production, standardization, differentiation, competition, marketing etc., enter in the picture as crucial determinants in shaping the nature and contents of the texts.

The texts in television are produced under conditions similar in nature to that of any other unit of the culture industry. The texts are telecast to a wide spectrum of audience as programmes. A wide variety of programmes on different themes are telecast regularly, though they are supposed to contain only cultural genres. With "overwhelming but insignificant variety of products on offer", the situation in TV as Steinert puts "is like that of a supermarket".[1] It is all the more so because, as many as 200 and odd channels produce and relay programmes which can be selected by consumers as and when they like. Such programmes thus constitute the product mix of television industry. The purpose of this chapter is to uncover the complexion of the programmes of television in India, and to delineate the contours of their contents.

Changing Complexion of Programme Mix in India

During the formative days of TV, very few programmes were telecast as the duration of transmission itself was for one or two hours a day. The programmes began to enlarge with the extension of transmission time and with the inclusion of entertainment programmes. By 1990, the coverage of TV comprised 43,38 hours of transmission time in an year encompassing a wide variety of progrmmes. Table 5.1 gives the percentage distribution of time for different categories of programmes.

Table 5.1: Percentage Share of Different Programmes in 1990

Name of the Programme	*Per cent*
A. Information Programmes	
1. News bulletin	11.5
2. Other information programmes	2.1
Total of A	13.6
B. Educational Programmes	
1. Related to specific curriculum	13.4
2. For rural development	10.5
3. Other educational programmes	15.7
4. Cultural pogrammes	8.1
5. Religious programmes	—
6. Advertisements	0.7
Total of B	48.4
C. Entertainment Programmes	
1. Cinemas and films	10.4
2. Plays	15.3
3. Music performance	5.4
4. Sports programmes	5.8
5. Other entertainments	1.1
Total of C	38.0
Grand Total (A + B + C)	**100.0**

Note: cultural programmes and advertisements are included under educational programmes by UNESCO for reasons not disclosed.
Source: *UNESCO Yearbook 1994.*[2]

As can be seen from the Table, a wide variety of programmes were telecast in 1990. They can be broadly divided into three categories viz: informative, educational and entertainment programmes. Since television was promoted for development purposes during its formative days, practically all the programmes were development oriented in nature with educational and instructive contents. It was only in 1976, that TV became commercial by introducing entertainment progrmmes which began to grow in size and importance since then. As can be seen from the Table entertainment programmes could account for 38 per cent of the transmission time by 1990. On the other hand, entertainments accounted for 77.3 per cent in Australia, 54 per cent in Canada, 62 per cent in Italy, 53.4 per cent in Switzerland and so on.[3] Educational progrmmes formed the largest category in India. Different kinds of educational programmes including those relating to culture accounted for 48.6 per cent.

With the entry of private sector in broadcasting since 1990, there has been unprecedented growth in the number of channels in the country. Most of them are telecasting programmes all the 24 hours of the day. Naturally, the magnitude of broadcasting time runs into hundreds of thousands of hours. Most of the channels telecast almost all kinds of programmes. However, channels like DD Sports, Star Sports, The National Geographic Channel, CNN, Pogo, Animal Planet, The History Channel, SS Music, Discovery, etc. concentrate on specialized programmes. With the mushroom growth of channels, the calculation of actual proportion of time devoted to each category of programme is well nigh impossible. Since most of the private channels belong to the category of commercials, the percentage of time for entertainment would be much higher. Public broadcasting channels also allocate their schedules in favour of entertainment. The programme-mix of Doordarsan Kendra Thiruvananthapuram during the year 2007 was made up with 66 per cent for entertainment, 13 for education and 21 per cent for information.[4] Tables 5.2 and 5.3 respectively give the typical programme chart of DD 1, the premier Public Broadcasting Channel and of Asianet one of the leading private channel in the south on a day in March 2007.

Table 5.2: Programme Schedule of DD 1

Time	*Name of the Programme*
06-55	Sanskrit Samachar
07-00 @ 20-00	Samachar/The News
07-30	Bhakti Aradhana
8-00	World Cup Highlights
9-00	North East Roundup
9-30	Yeh Gulsta Hamara
10-00	SAARC Summit Opening Ceremony Live
12-30, 00-30	Stree Teri Kahani
13-00	Pap Punya Ka Lekha Jokha
13-30	Kashmakesh Zindigi Ki
14.-00	Apna Mere Apna
14-30	Jaayan Kahani
15-00	Ek Kahani
15-30	Shahn
1600	Healthy India
17-30	Evening Live Show
18-00	Punjabi Darpa
18-30	Krishi Darshan
18-45	Grameen Bharat
19-00	Metro News
19-15	Kavi Mosti Mushira
20-30	Sanskar
21-00	Sohni Mahiwal
21-30	Lal Kohni Alvida
22-00	Jo Kahunga Sach Kahunga
23-00	Bioscope Hum Apke Hain Kaun (serialized feature)

Source: *The Hindu* dated 24-3-2007.[5]

Thus the list covers altogether 26 programmes scheduled for that day. The programme schedule consists of news, sports, development programmes, entertainment programmes. With minor variations, programmes for the other days also correspond to this pattern. Being a public service broadcasting channel, DD 1 is bound to give priority to programmes designed to promote the welfare of the country than to secure commercial gains. In addition to DD 1, Doordarshan is having special channels for sports, culture, news and so on. Doordarshan has also to reconcile the national and regional interests while airing its programmes. Naturally, DD 1 concentrates on themes of national importance, leaving themes of local and regional importance to various regional channels.

Private channels also follow the same with minor variations in the pattern of their programmes (see Table 5.3) Thus there were 31 programmes scheduled for that day. The schedule comprises informative, instructional and entertainment programmes. Tele-serials and movies form the important entertainment programmes. Though there is not much difference with the programmes of DD 1, the channel is guided by commercial considerations. Unlike DD, profit motive rather than national commitment takes precedence in scheduling the programmes. Other private channels follow the pattern of Asianet in arranging their programmes. Channels located in different regions specialise in programmes suitable to those regions and present them in the respective regional language. Thus, Sun presents in Tamil, Zee in Hindi, Enadu in Telugu and so on. All India channels and foreign channels broadcast programmes both in English and Hindi.

Contents of the Programmes

News

Conveyance of news is one of the foremost functions of television. Television has become the source of news to more than 75 per cent of the people in most of the advanced countries of the world. According to the National Readership Survey, the number of people watching television is more than the number of people reading newspapers in our country.[6] Apparently, television is the source of news for more than half the number of people in India also. All the channels except the specialized channels like sports or music telecast news regularly in the morning, afternoon and evening. In addition to the regular news, documentaries and discussions of current affairs are occasionally telecast. The main attraction of television stems from its capacity to telecast news as and when any event takes place. Naturally, one needs not wait for the next day for getting the news as in the case of newspaper. In fact, "live television reporting introduces an immediacy missing in the print media".[7]

Table 5.3: List of Programmes of Asianet

Time	*Items of Programme*
06-0	Rangamalika
06-30	Devageetham
06-55, 07-30 & 08-30	Asianet Peradhana Varthakal
07-0	Nithyanantham
07-35	Suprabatham
09-00	Kannadi
09-30	Cinema Dairy
10-00	Filmi Thamasha
10-30	Puthiyageethangal
11-00	WWS
11-30	Samayam
12-00	Swarnamamayooram
12-30	Stree oru Santhanam
13-00 & 22-30	Asianet Varthkal
13-30	Chambakulam Thachan (movie)
16-30	Valkannadi
17-35	Sayhannam
17-55	Swantham Suryaputri
18-25, 23	Munshi
18-30	News lime
19-00	Malayogam
19-30	Nonbarappuve
20-00	Ammamanasu
20-30	Samadooram
21-00	Pavithra Jajjilnu
21-30	Swami Ayyappan
22-00	Sanmanasullavarkku Samadhanam
23-05	Lulu Gulf Round up
23-35	Five Star Thattukada
00-05	SIB Quiz
00-30	Gulf Varthakal

Source: *The Hindu* dated 24th March, 2007.

Certain principles are involved in the preparation of news. News forms an event which has to be gathered and processed. What categories of events have to be treated as a fit item to be processed as news is one question posed in this connection. They have to be filterd as and when they are presented by the gatekeepers and processed into presentational style. While preparing them as news, the personal bias of the editor has to be avoided in order to maintain the news value. Similarly, exaggerated versions should be avoided and a balanced presentation should be preserved. At the same time, the background of the event, the implication of the event etc., should be appropriately incorporated to get a clear picture. Visuals of the event accompanying the news make them more attractive.

News itself falls into four categories viz.; world, national, regional and local. The problem with world news is that the majority of events are not directly relevant to the lives of those who watch them. Similarly, local news may not be interested to a large number of audience. Careful demarcation of the different categories should be maintained in the presentation of the four categories. It has become an accepted practice with many regional channels to give special weight to local news during recent years. *Nattuvartha* (local news) as it is called in Malayalam, forms a separate category of news programme with many channels.

Of late, news is very often presented in a form known as tabloid news. In tabloid news, sensational items are being projected for the purpose of attracting the attention of the audience. They do not display journalistic values, but entertain the audiences with scandals, gossips, and celebrites, etc. as the standard fare. In the language of journalism, they fall within what is is termed yellow journalism. Credit should go to the channels in India for not imitating the example of other countries in showing undue importance to tabloid news.

Investigating journalism is a new development associated with the news programmes of television. Events of topical importance or of sensational in nature are probed further to find out the forces or the background behind such events. In some cases, they could unearth the true picture behind such events. One of the important events in which the culprits could be brought to justice by the active involvement of TV in our country is the Jessica murder case. However, investigating journalism can go to the extent of breaking the private life of persons involved or suspected to be involved in such cases. It may also create embarrassing situations to the victims. As an author puts "too much investigative programming leads not to truth, simply to viewer desensitization and exhaustion".[8]

Very often, it can be embarrassing to the concerned parties as for example, of what happened during the American hostages crisis following the Iranian revolution of the late 1970s on account of the continuous pressure exerted on the relatives of the hostages by the reporters for collecting news. As Harless enjoins many of the relatives-obviously innocent bystanders-felt that they were grilled even by more polite reporters.[9] With the proliferation of channels, such scenarios are on the increase in India also. The tendency with some private channels seems to be to twist the facts and to present an exaggerated version of events. In a state like Kerala, where political consciousness is very strong, such versions of news get popular approval even with the educated classes.

One new development in the news programme is the inclusion of entertainment as an integral part of the news. Interestingly, the word story stands for the contents of news in the jargon of the media. Actually, as an author puts, the journalists supply "stories that offer entertainment to the audience"[10] rather than inform people. Nobody writes a news report deliberately to make it uninteresting or dull. Instead, he writes as lively and interestingly as possible. The kind of news that attracts most of the readers and viewers is news that is entertaining and appealing to their emotions than to the mind.[11] Of late, such a twist has become glaring in the reporting of major events in our country also. As an author put it, the live coverage" "tilts completely towards the hyper mould of reality show, adding to it aspects of film at will for untold entertainment" with an eye for earning more money through advertisement.[12]

Another important development pertaining to news relates to the presentation of analysis of news or discussions on current affairs very often with a panel of experts. Even news per se is moving into this direction. The impact of the news on socio-economic life or culture or political repercussions are explored or even speculated. Critics maintain that most of such discussions in India lack credibility and objectivity.[13] Very often people entrusted with the preparation of such programmes do not have sufficient experience and competence to conduct such discussions. A typical example is the live discussion on the budget. Almost all the channels vigorously undertake such discussions. Invariably, most of the so called experts whom the channels engage for the discussion are mere novices who do not even have any idea of what the budget is or the economic scenario of the country. As and when the finance minister makes a statement, they will start harping on this or that aspect without having any clear idea about the issues involved. Nevertheless, some of the channels like NDTV present such programmes with high standards and skill.

Educational and Development Programmes

Television was introduced in India as a tool to promote the ongoing process of development of the country. In those days, the leaders of the country and policy makers believed that television can be effectively used for diffusing the development message in the remote corners of the country. Accordingly, programmes were designed in such a way as to foster the various development schemes and also to eradicate social evils like dowry, child marriage, superstition, caste rigidity etc. Curriculum programmes for the school children and those with themes for development were telecast. In the opinion of Mitra, "television was conceived as a tool that would become the centre around which an entire instructional institution would develop".[14]

Most of such programmes seem to have proved unpopular with very little tangible results. The declining popularity of those educational broadcasts of the formative days paved the way for broadening the scope and style of educational programmes. Textual strategies like talk shows, quiz and game shows and dramatization took precedence over the regular curriculum based programmes. Among them talk shows involving discussion on a particular issue by a set of experts and hosts were given more prominence. Talk shows for youth, children and women became another category. While women's programmes revolved around the challenges they face in India, youth programmes were concerned with the questions that are pertinent to the emerging youth culture. The approach in children's programme has been to deal with issues that are of interest to youngsters. This stylistic balance with emphasis on development was retained even after the introduction of commercials in 1976. No wonder, nearly 50 per cent of the programmes were for development or educational purposes before the entry of private channels in 1990. However, on the other hand educational programmes could account for a very low percentage of the programmes in most of the developed countries. It was for example, only 10.2 per cent in Canada, 1.2 per cent in Italy, 2.2 per cent in Germany and 4.1 per cent in Australia and so on in 1990.[15] The importance assigned to educational and developmental themes began to decline with the entry of private channels in 1990s. Even Doordarshan seems to be disinclined to give undue importance to the development oriented programmes. Nevertheless, some of the programmes of Doordarshan, like *Grameen Bharat*, Eucational programmes of UGC and IGNOU are also being telecast regularly. Similarly, *Krishi Darshan* carries development message in our country. Some of the programmes like *Haritha Keralam*, Hello Doctor of the regional channels are also impregnated with development themes. Nevertheless, developmental and educational themes have become a marginalised category among the programmes in our country.

Entertainment Programmes

Entertainment programmes constitute the third category. They have gained prominence at the expense of educational programmes even with Doordarshan. In this context, what Edison had observed on the transformation of cinema as an entertainment medium has become true in the case of television also. His observation was; "I had some glowing dreams about what the camera could be made to do and ought to do in teaching the world the things it needed to know-teaching in a more vivid direct way—I am disappointed that it has been turned out into an entertainment toy".[16] Similarly, much against the dreams of many scholars and policy makers, television has also become a channel catering mainly to the entertainment needs in almost all the countries of the world. In fact, some of the channels devoted to specialised programmes have also turned to entertainment programmes in a big way. The former Christian Broadcasting Network now called the Family Channel for instance, has switched its programming signals from religious to entertainment fare. Similarly, the Nickelodeon, the Arts Entertainment Network, the Discovery Channel etc. are progressively turning to entertainment programmes[17]. In our country also the ascendancy of entertainment programmes has gained momentum with the entry of private channels. A wide variety of programmes fall within the ambit of entertainment. They themselves can be broadly divided into primary and secondary categories. The primary category includes tele-serials, soap operas, sitcoms, dramas, and film based progrmmes like regular movies, chitrahar etc. Programmes like sports, games, quizzes etc. fall within the ambit of the second category. Cookery programmes, religious programmes etc. are also broadcast regularly in the TV. Though they are not entertainment programmes per se, they represent certain cultural practices or activities. They can therefore be classified within the broader category of entertainment progammes.

It is the presence of entertainment programmes in a big way which entitles television to be reckoned as a branch of the culture industry and which is concerned with the production of texts embodying creative contents connoting symbolic meanings. They meet the human urge for entertainment and amusement, very essential conditions for leading a contented life. The unprecedented growth of television stems primarily because of its capacity to cater to the needs of people for entertainment which is met with a wide variety of programmes. In turn, the entertainment programmes like tele-serials, soap operas, movies etc. colonise practically the entire prime time of TV schedules, apparently on account of their popular appeal. However, what television offers to man are nothing but "the stone of stereotypes" as Adorno and Horkheimer sarcastically put. In their opinion, culture industry is corrupt "not because it is sinful Babylon, but because it is a cathedral dedicated to elevated pleasure."[18]

In the Western countries, most of the genres of entertainment programmes were evolved during the experimental years of the 1960s and 1970s. According to an author, it is difficult to make novelty from a pre-determined framework especially because producers are reluctant to make changes from the established format primarily on account of the budgetary constraints and stiff competition.[19] Programmes in India follow the same formats with slight modifications. Thus tele-serials, soaps, sitcoms and movies find prominent place among the entertainment programmes in India also.

Among the entertainment programmes in India, tele-serials are perhaps the most important. In shaping the tele-serials, elements of two formats, theatre and feature films- are incorporated liberally. During the initial days, the television play remained a broadcast of stage theatre without the use of any specific televisional style. However, with the further improvements in technology, a new style or format in the presentation could take shape. In the words of Mitra "as technique matured, the notions of visual space and light were reexamined and plays were transformed into tele-plays where multiple cameras, shot/reverse shot, eyre-line matching a variety of other textual strategies were used to develop the tele-play as a well-defined set of programs".[20] Moreover, tele-plays could bring actors and actresses much closer to the audience.

The incorporation of cinematic format is much more deep in the tele-serials. Many factors account for this deeper influence of films on television serials. Basically television is only a technological improvement of the cinematic technique. No wonder, television serials follow cinematic formats. As in films, producers are reluctant to deviate from the accepted or successful formulas. Formating of the stars is another method adopted from films. Television has also adopted the music-dance formula which is very popular with the Indian movies.

A far more important reason for the influence of films is the presence of a large number of ex-film artistes in the making of tele-series. In fact, it was the ex-film people like Ramesh Sippy, or Chopra who started the ball rolling.[21] What happened was the large scale entry of film people with their genres and formats especially as film industry began to decline with the entry of television as an entertainment medium. At present many ex-film stars also appear in TV serials. In Malayalam serials for example, Sheela, Sidiqui, Seema, Sukumari, Nedumudi Venu, Balachandra Menon, Ganesh, Devan, Janardhanan, the late Murali, K.P.A.C. Lalitha, late Sri Vidya are only a few stars who have appeared as leading artists. Nevertheless, a whole generation of fine artistes have grown around television which provides a forum for the young artists to display their talents.

With the theatre cum film background, tele-serials could command high popularity in India. Almost all the channels vie with each other in telecasting serials after serials during prime time. Excepting a few minutes earmarked for news, practically the entire time from 6-10 in the in the evenings is scheduled for serials. They in turn comprise a large number of episodes each with their internal closure but with a continuity which induces the audience to watch the following episode.[22]

Much before the formation of tele-serials as a form of entertainment programme. another format had arrived in India from foreign lands. It is the soap opera, an important genre which had its origin in the US during the formative days of television. Basically, it is another version of tele-serials. Soap spread to the European countries and South America in quick succession. While British and American soaps are associated with female audience, the South American version, telenovela's appeal is to audience across class and gender divide. It is so popular in South America that the networks there broadcast nine to fourteen tele-novelas for five to six days in every week. While British soaps orient around realistic themes, those of American origin take a melodramatic form.

According to Baker, soaps are a specific genre of television not only in their narrative form but also in their pivotal themes which centre on the sphere of interpersonal relationships. As he adds further "marriages, divorces, break-ups and coming together, alliances, arguments, acts of revenge and acts of caring are at the core of soap opera".[23] In soaps, as an author puts, the audiences suffer, enjoy, and laugh with the things that are happening on the screen as if they were happening to themselves. Invariably, soap watching is an absorbing but relaxing and comforting experience. Soaps create a sense of community feeling. Soaps encompass issues of fidelity, and adultery, generational conflicts, mere gossip, family tension, love hatred, indifference, violence, sexual attractions, normal neurosis, and other sentiments.[24] The paradigmatic structure of soaps itself is the presentation of never ending narratives with each episode presenting an unanswered question. As in the case of tele-serials, soap episodes running for months instill a sense of continuity.

It reached India when commercials were introduced in 1980s. Beginning with the first soap opera, *Hum Log* in 1984-85 there was as Singhal puts, "a programme revolution in Doordarshan".[25] *Hum Log* was followed by *Buniyad* a historical soap opera, and Ramayana and Mahabharat, two epic cum religious operas. It is claimed that Mahabhrat could entrance 300 million audience for an hour every Sunday for 20 months. Even now soap operas, especially those that portray the tension between mothers-in-law and daughters-in-law remain the most popular shows.[26]

Television channels all over the country have been producing and broadcasting a wide variety of serials and soap operas in Hindi and other regional languages since 1990s. Most of them run for months. As a genre, they have become a hot favourite both with men and women alike. In a city like Trivandrum for instance, as one reporter has stated "men— are gradually catching the soap opera fever".[27] Serials like *Jwalayayi Stree, Sanmanasullavarkku Samadhanam, Ente ManasaPutri, Orethuvalpakshi* etc., have made headlines in Kerala. The storylines of most of the serials are loosely parallel revolving around marriage and family though some of them contain attempts to shock the audiences with rapes, extramarital affairs. conspiracies, kidnappings and even murders. However, serials which could gain classical stature seem to be scarce if not nil. Of late, there seems to be an erosion in the popularity of teleserials.

The entertainment programmes modeled after cinematic themes are not the only category of cinematic items scheduled in TVs. Instead, films and film based entertainments are regularly telecast in all the channels. At least one movie is being relayed every day in each channel. Since the high cost of production of movies cannot be easily recouped by broadcasting through TV, channels do not telecast pictures immediately after release. Instead, what they do is to acquire broadcast rights of old films which are popular and then to telecast them. Another popular programmes have been Chitrahar, a film based dance music programme.[28] In such programmes, television is able to present the visual image of the dance accompanied by the song along with the actors and actresses. Compared to the pictures in colour TV, mere music and dance programmes are lifeless. In sum, the influence of film on TV is deep rooted. Though the growth of television has adversely affected film industry, it could retain its hold on the entertainment world through its direct or indirect influence on the serials and other formats of TV.

Nevertheless, the manner in which entertainment is being promoted is not free from criticism. Very often, entertainment programmes project sexy scenes and violent behaviour without any inhibition. As Williams enjoins "it is doubtful whether before the epoch of television serials and series anything like the current proportion of dramatic attention to crime and illness had ever existed".[29] Such a pattern seems to have grown as an outcome of the influence of films on TV. "Many of the films except a few ones which are comedies" as Bhatt puts "show us half a dozen or more murders being committed by the villain and his gang until a Bachchen or Shroff puts paid to his depradations and the police are brought in towards the climax".[30] Most of the tele-serials blindly imitate this pattern without any hesitation and each channel broadcasts daily episodes of four or five serials containing such violent scenes. Some of them show scenes of cruel murder and violence against women with impunity.

Similarly, projection of sex is another legacy inherited from films. As in films, the producers of serials also insist on their heroines and other females "to bare their legs, backs, part of the breast as much as the censors would wink at" As Bhatt enjoins further; "The display of sex is is not confined to the baring of the the vital parts of the body only". Other performances like "songs and dances have over the past few years become exercises in pelvic pushes, the hero falling on and rolling on the the floor or grass with the heroine, hero and heroine in deep embrace, hero kissing various parts of heroines body and so on". Needless to say, the display of such exercises kindle sexual instincts in the minds of the spectators.[31] Even most of the so called family serials are full of such sexy scenes. The usual techniques like rain and thunder, switching off the light, snuggling behind the scenes, drawing up the sheets, etc. suggestive of physical intimacy are common in them. At least in some serials kisses on the lips and other seductive scenes are also not uncommon. As Page and Williams maintain, many soap operas have modelled themselves on the sexual openness of American soap operas.[32] It was only the other day (March, 2007) programmes of one channel FTV was banned for the display of immoral scenes. Entertainment programmes of such a nature can certainly be harmful to the society. Though scholars differ as to the extent of harmful effects of such scenes on the behavioural pattern of people at large, they are sure to carry a bad impression in the minds of young children. Bhat exposes a particular scene of how sexual impression is created in the mind of an innocent child in graphic terms thus: "In Dard, a family serial on DD Metro, a small six-year looking son of a heroine who has married a much older man, calls her 'sexy' when the old father is also present. She tries to drive some sense into him by asking him whether he knew the meaning of the word sexy and equally promptly the reply comes that he picked it up from Govinda the hero who sang that song in the film referred to. That the actress playing the heroine is also the producer of the serial makes her intention clear, while the sexy craze lasts why not exploit it in one's serial".[33] Such serials themselves testify the bad image created in the minds of young children. They may not be embarrassing to see such scenes alone in a room. It will however, be embarrassing to see such scenes in the company of children and other members of the family. Some exponents of violent scenes and indecent exposure of sex maintain that they are only creative expressions of artistic freedom. If it were to be so, they should be tolerated, if not promoted. However, a closer examinations of such scenes indicates that such scenes do not contain any artistic expression of creativity. In fact, they are in a sense exhibitions of phonography meant to create erotic sensation.[34] Adorno who was very skeptical about culture industry, regards them as a deceptive illusion.[35] All such exploits are done for the purpose of attracting attention of the audience and thereby making money. As Mullan puts, "they are formulaic commercial products made for profit".[36]

Dramas, sitcoms and documentaries are other forms of entertainment programmes. As a matter of fact, most of the genres in television, whether it be in the shape of soaps, movies or tele-serials are basically dramatic in character. Actually the rise of serialized dramatic themes has resulted in the decline of single play. They were very popular during the initial stages. With the entry of commercials, they have lost much of their glamour. Instead, detective serials are able to rise in popularity.[37] Sitcoms were popular kinds of entertainment in the past. They were popular apparently because, they humourously represented some small failings or eccentricity, mild misfortunes or problems of retirement, change of job, etc. Documentaries form another category of programmes which had its origin from the time of Lumiere films of 1890s. Documentaries which were very popular have been edged out by current affairs programmes.[38]

Sports

Sports are perhaps the most important entertainment programme next to tele-serials. While tele-serials and other cinematic formats fall within the ambit of culture in some way or other, sports cannot be regarded as a cultural activity proper. Nevertheless, sports are closely related to television from its formative days. In turn, channels like DD Sports, STAR Sports, ESPN, Ten Sports etc. which specialize in telecasting sports programmes have come into existence. Ordinary channels also include sports events as part of their schedule. Since the inception of television, sports events are reconstructed to fit the requirements of television. As Mullan enjoins over the past three decades television has altered the morning scheduling of West Coast Basket Ball to suit East Coast television, forced basket players to play world series games on freezing October evenings. Television has thus rearranged the sporting calendar and separated sports from their familiar relationships with natural season.[39]

Furthermore, television has contributed to the decline of some sports and to the rise of some others into prominence. Cricket matches for example, have shot into prominence and cricket fans have come into existence in most parts of the world thanks to the television coverage. Various other kinds of sport events like football, basket ball and athlete meets are relayed. Television could create a novel form of excitement and immediacy with various sports programmes by adjusting the camera. As Bignal puts: "The positioning of cameras in television coverage of sport provides a much closer view of the action than is normally available to spectators at the event itself, and cutting between camera shot allows the television viewer to identify with the efforts and emotions of the competitors".[40] At the same time, an instant commentary by gifted people could create new dimensions to the entertainment format of television. Not surprisingly, sports are progressively being transformed as an entertainment format on par with other formats. As Dave Hill, Head of Sky Sports remarked jocularly in 1991 "sport as drama and sport as soap opera—that is what people watch on television."[41]

One notable consequence in India is the transformation of cricket matches as events of national importance, watched by people all over the country. According to a study made by Nilu Damle in some villages of Maharastra "even in the village of Ekurka, a small village with no satellite TV, people are mad about cricket, thanks to televised cricket matches".[42] Similarly cricket players are being elevated as celebrites. Pattodies, Tendulkers, Gavaskers, Azharuddins, Kumblais and other cricketeers are in the lips of even kids of the kindergarten.

Side by side, the mutual dependence between sports and

television has become deep rooted. Sports men could not only emerge as celebrites but also command huge volume of money as reward channeled through television. As a matter of fact, television provides huge volume income which gate receipt and sponsorship alone could never command.[43] In turn, the channels thrive with the inflow of advertisement revenue by sponsoring sports events.

Quiz and games programme form another category of entertainment. They have their origin in Victorian parlour games, fairground side shows and popular activities like bingo. Almost all the channels conduct quiz programmes in India. Quiz masters like Siddartha Basu could gain world wide recognition by their quiz programmes of superb quality. Cookery forms a new category of programmes which have gained importance during recent years. Almost all the channels vie with each other in presenting new forms of cookery formulas. Women audiences listen with apt attention cookery programmes showing how different varieties of dishes are prepared in various parts of India. Almost all the channels telecast religious programmes also. Side by side, channels exclusively broadcasting religious programmes also operate in India. With the rise of religious fundamentalism, religious programmes are having high receptivity in our country.

Reality Shows

A new form of entertainment programme termed reality show has shot into prominence during recent years. Technological inventions like those of digital camera and internet which facilitate interactive participation can be stated to be instrumental to the evolution of the new format in which elements of fictional narratives and documentaries are appropriated. The declining importance of tele-serials as prime-time entertainment progrmme stands as an equally important reason for the emergence of the reality shows.

What is new in the reality show is the purported presentation of real life situation, in the place of the fictional elements. A wide variety of programmes comprising talent hunts, game shows, celebrity shows, documentary-style shows, or mere plain voyeurism personified etc., fall within the rubric of reality shows. Since reality shows are still in an evolving stage, a clear picture demarcating its boundaries cannot be easily drawn. In fact, the boundaries between real and fiction get blurred in many cases. Most of the unscripted entertainments, genres of real people, sports, political debates, documentaries and even dog shows are labeled as reality shows. However, authors like Andrejevics confine to genres which rely on comprehensive surveillance of daily lives and unscripted interactions of people who agree to participate in making their private lives public, for the purpose of uncovering the implications of reality shows.[44] The possibility for interaction and participation in the programme is the great merit of reality shows. While the usual top-down TV programmes from above, relegate the audience to the level of mere passive spectators, reality shows elevate them as active partners in the making of the contents of the progrmmes,. By ensuring democratic participation, it offers, as an author enjoins the possibility for making stars out of real people.[45] Programmes are created for the people by the people. There is thus a devolution of power from the producer to the consumer. In a sense, it is akin to the transfer of tools and means of production to the workers as visualized by Marx.

Another great merit of reality show is the low cost of production. At a time when commercial channels find it hard to turn out quality programmes at high cost, reality shows can be turned out at one third of the cost of fiction centered serials. Apparently they provide a viable alternative to the growing number of channels to withstand the competition in the market.

Notwithstanding the purported merits, reality shows actually demonstrate the artificial character of mediated reality and highlight the reality of artifice in the mass media.[46] In such a situation, what is transpired in it is only a reflection of the emerging reality of the interactive economy. Looking from this angle, reality TV serves the interests of the producers in an environment wrought about by the interactive technology. In so doing, they become some form of marketing instrument with very little regard to artistic qualities. In fact, as the producer of

Survivor concedes "My shows create an interest, and people will look at them, but the endgame here is selling products in stores—a car, deodorant, running shooes".[47] In other words, instead of empowering the viewers as partners, viewer participation is designed merely to promote the interests of the producers by reducing costs and rationalizing both production and marketing. An unholy alliance between the channels and the sponsors seems to be widespread in the entire scenario. Ipsofacto, the much orchestrated active participation of the audience becomes a doubtful proposition. By and large, what Hesmondhalgh states about digital television in general holds squarely good in the case of reality show. He states thus; "And for all the rhetoric of choice and interactivity, much of it derived from internet-speak, digital television very much remains the centralized, top-down medium that developed in the era of analogue telecasting".[48]

It is a moot point whether reality shows can be treated as cultural products. The absence of symbolic element in most of the reality shows weakens their claim to be counted as cultural products. On the other hand, if culture in the broader sense connoting it as the way of life of a people is taken as the criterion, reality shows also fit in as products of culture as they endeavour to reflect life in the real form. At the same time, they provide a platform for any citizen to express his artistic skills and talents. In this respect, they are very close to sports which also form a unit of culture industry. Being an instrument for expressing life in real form, they can be regarded as the latest form of artistic creation. In fact, an author claims that the advent of reality show is as important for our time as were the inventions of drama and novel for earlier generations.[49]

Reality show has become a leading genre dominating the ratings during prime-time. The ratings of reality shows are stated to be very high. It is reported that more than 45 per cent of the audience watch reality shows in the US and one fifth of them have become die-hard fans or addicts of such programmes. Furthermore, the youngsters in the age group 18-24 form the bulk of the audience.[50] Some of the reality shows like the *Big Brother, The American Family, Temptation Island,*

Survivor, Who Wants to be a Millionaire etc. could make hits in the US.

Close on the heels of the Western channels, Indian channels have also ventured into the realm of reality programmes with suitable modifications to Indian conditions. Talent hunt of Channel V for making a musical band involving a group of girls is believed to be the beginning of reality TV in India. Since then, reality shows began to appear one after another. Amitabh Bachchan's *Kaun Banega Krorpati*, an Indian version of *Who Wants to be a Millionaire* was a notable hit among reality shows in India. The *Indian Idol* with boys next door turning into singing sensation, *Big Boss* the Indian version of *UK's Big Brother, Nach Baliye involving celebrity couples* battling against each otherin dance competition, *Jodi Number One* an Indian reality dance show, *Ustaadon Ka Ustaad* a talent show of stars from other shows compete with each other in singing, dancing and comedy routines and so on are some of the other notable reality shows at the all India level.[51] Most of the shows in India are competition shows in dancing or singing. Shows on real life situation seem to be rare if not absent. The regional channels in Malayalam, Tamil or Telugu have not been far behind in introducing reality shows. They also follow the all India pattern.

Notwithstanding the popularity of reality shows, and the chances they provide for ordinary people to develop their talents, they safeguard business interests in a subtle way. The critics in India feel that participation of real people seems to be negligible if not nil in most of the reality shows. In many cases, the influential few dominate the whole exercise. One reader went to the extent of stating that the reality behind the reality shows is that there is no reality at all in them. Instances like that of Shijini Sen Gupta collapsing after being humiliated by the judges in a Bengali reality show are not isolated cases.[52] Since they are in the nascent form, an depth analysis is yet to take place.

Conclusion

A plethora of programmes are being telecast by the hundreds and odd channels everyday in our country. With the help of cable, audience can select any one programme of their choice. The emergence of reality show facilitates the audience to participate in the programmes and even interact with the stars. Notwithstanding the possibility of turning out different forms of art in their pristine beauty, the only form of genre which has emerged with TV is the tele-serials. However, it has transformed itself as a pure commercial product catering mainly to the entertainment needs of the people. Even otherwise, TV has to operate on commercial lines as production of any programme involves high cost of production. The products have therefore to be marketed at least for recouping the cost of production. In turn, it has grown as a money making business with the norms of marketing governing the whole process. How television markets its products and makes money forms the theme of the next chapter.

NOTES AND REFERENCES

1. Heinz, Steinert (2003). *Culture Industry,* Translated by Sally-Ann Spencer Cambridge, Polity Press, p. 102.
2. UNESCO (1994). *Statistical yearbook,* 1994.
3. UNESCO (1994). *op. cit.*
4. Prasar Bharati (2007). *Doordarshan Kendra Thiruvananthapuram A Profile.*
5. *The Hindu* dated 24-3-2007.
6. National Readership Study 2006; see *The Hindu* dated Aug 30th for a summary of the report.
7. David, Page and William, Crawley (2001). *Satellite over South Asia: Broadcasting Culture and the Public Interest,* London, Sage Publication.
8. Mullan Bob (1997). *Consuming Television,* Oxford, Blackwell Publishers, p. 49.
9. James, Harless (1990). *Mass Communication: An Introductory Survey,* Dubuque, Wmc. Publishers, p. 359.
10. Herbert, Altschull (1995). *Agents of Power: The Media and Public Policy,* New York Longman, p. 124.
11. Herbert, Altschull (1995). *op. cit.,* p. 123.
12. Padmanabhan, Chitra "Television news is for reel" in *The Hindu* dated 2-1-2009.
13. Rajagopalan, V. (2000). *Television Journalism* (Mal), Kottayam, Current Books, p. 88.

14. Mitra, Anand (1993). *Television in India: A Study of Mahabharat*, Delhi, Sage Publications, p. 79.
15. UNESCO *Yearbook* 1995.
16. Quoted by Robert Wagner in "The Motion Picture in US Education" in Donald Staples (ed). *The American Cinema*, Washington DC, Voice of American Forum Series 1973, p. 343.
17. Blumber Jay, G. (1991). "The New Television Market Place, Imperatives Implications and Issues" in James Curran and Michael Gurevitch (ed). *Mass Media and Society*, London, Edward Arnold; A Division of Hodder and Stonghton, p. 207.
18. Adorno, T.W. and Horkheimer, Max (1977). "Culture Industry: Enlightenment as Mass Deception" in J. Curran (ed.) *Mass Communication and Society*, London, Open University, p. 365.
19. Mullan, Bob, *op. cit.*, p. 42.
20. Mitra, Anand (1993), *op. cit.*, p. 82.
21. Bhatt, S.C. (1994). *Satellite Invasion of India*, New Delhi, Gyan Publishing House, p. 152.
22. Mitra, Aand (1993). *op. cit.*, p. 86.
23. Baker, Chris (1997). *Global Television: An Introduction*, Oxford, Blackwell Publishers, p. 79.
24. Mullan, Bob. *op. cit.*, p. 52.
25. Singhal, Arvind and Everett, M. Rogers (2001). *India's Communication Revolution; from Bullock Carts to Cyber Marts*, New Delhi, Sage Publications, p. 90.
26. Article entitled "How the World Watches Television" in the *The Hindu* 20th June, 2007.
27. Liz, George in *The Hindu* dated 24-5-2006.
28. Mitra, Anand (1993). *op. cit.*, p. 84.
29. Williams, Raymond (1990). *Television: Technology and Cultural Form*, London, Routledge, p. 60.
30. Bhatt, S.C. (1993). *op. cit.*, p. 154.
31. Bhatt, S.C. (1993). *op. cit.*, p. 156.
32. David, Page and William, Crawley (2001). *op. cit.*, p. 163.
33. Bhatt, S.C. (1993). *op. cit.*, p. 157.
34. Bob, Mullan (1997). *op. cit.*, p. 137.
35. Steinert quotes from Adorno. see Heinz, Steinert (2003). *op. cit.*, p. 103.
36. Bob, Mullan (1997). *op. cit.*, p. 137.
37. Bob, Mullan (1997). *op. cit.*, p. 60.
38. Bob, Mullan (1997). *op. cit.*, p. 48.
39. Bob, Mullan (1997). *op. cit.*, p. 57.
40. Jonathan, Bignell (2004). *An Introduction of Television Studies*, London, Routledge, p. 265.
41. Barnett, Steven (1998) quotes this passage in "Sport" in Anthony Smith (ed.) *Television: An International History*, Oxford University Press, p. 95.

42. Quoted by David, Page and William, Crawley (2001). *op. cit.* from the report on the study made by Nilu Damle on Latur District in May 1998, p. 162.
43. Barnett, Steven (1998). "Sport" in Smith Anthony (ed.), *Television An International History*, Oxford, Oxford University Press, p. 96.
44. Andrejevic, Mark (2004). *Reality TV; The Working of Being* Watched, Rowman and Littlefield Publishers Ltd., INC, p. 64.
45. Andrejevic, Mark (2004). *op. cit.*, p. 10.
46. Andrejevic, Mark (2004). *op. cit.*, p. 16.
47. The statement of Mike Sager is from Burnett Mark's "What I h've learned: Mark Burnett" in *Esquire* 136, July 2001. Andrejevic, Mark (2004) quotes it. See p. 43, of *op. cit.*
48. Hesmondhalgh, David (2002). *The Cultural Industries*, Sage Publications, p. 228.
49. Quoted by Andrejevic, Mark (2004). from Margaret Mead, p. 64, *op. cit.*
50. Andrejevic, Mark (2004) *op. cit.*, p. 9.
51. Manohar, Uttara (2007). "Reality TV: Reality Shows in India" (www. Buzzle.com/articles).
52. *The Hindu*. Kerala News, 12th July , 2008; "Reality shows; perils and positives abound".

6

How TV Markets its Products

Programmes with their roots in culture are produced on factory lines with the aid of highly advanced technology. Production itself is a complex process, which involves the services of different inputs including labour calling for high cost not only in production but also in transmission. Marketing becomes inevitable at least for recouping the cost, let alone to make any profit. Being a new kind of industry in which artistic genres and economic norms coalesce, the marketing system would be differing very much from that of the ordinary goods and services. How production is organized and marketing is undertaken, what are the peculiarities thereon and how channels earn income from marketing etc., form the theme of this chapter.

Organization of Production Units

Any TV channel which produces programmes and telecasts them is organized as a corporate enterprise and operates on commercial lines. Some of them operate as affiliates to multinational corporations or other business enterprises as in the case of STAR TV. Indian channels also operate as affiliates to other business concerns. A typical example is Zee television to which not less than 15 channels are affilited and at the same time it is connected to various other business enterprises. Even the regional channel, Manorama News is an affiliate of the Malayalam Daily, Malayala Manorama. Each of such channels is organized with different branches comprising production, engineering, marketing departments and the likes. These departments are in charge of different functions of the channel. In addition to the regular channels, the organizational structure of the industry includes programme makers who produce serials and other programmes and cables and satellites which facilitate the smooth conveyance of the programmes to the consumers in the households. Needless to say, huge amounts of capital are invested in such enterprises. Capital is needed to secure costly machines and equipments required to prepare the programmes and to telecast them. Working capital is also needed for operational expenses, administrative purposes and so on.

We are giving below the accounts of the costs and returns of two channels operating in Kerala to illustrate the modus operandi of the industry. One is a medium sized regional channel in Kerala, which we call channel A, was started with an authorized capital of Rs. 350 million.[1] The recurring cost needed for the production and telecasting of programmes of the channel amounts to millions of rupees. Another channel, which we call B was started with a share capital of Rs. 2,59,759,927.[2] It also incurred huge amounts of money for the preparation and telecasting of programmes. Table 6.1 indicates the details of various items of expenditure incurred by channel A in the year 2005-06.

Table 6.1: Statement of the Recurring Costs and Returns of Channel A for the Year 2005-06

Name of the Item of Cost	*Amount Rs.*
A. Items of Cost	
1. Programme production and software	1,96,19,041
2. News gathering	80,36,024
3. Uplinking charges	1,91,05,645
4. Equipment hire charges	31,50,287
5. Salaries and wages including provident fund	1,04,83,472
6. Administrative and other expenses	83,24,006
7. Interest and bank charges	47,48,036
Total of A	7,34,66,511
B. Returns	
1. Advertisement sales	3,21,85,919
2. Slot sales	1,46,33,219
3. Other income	7,60,201
Total of B	4,75,79,339
A-B	-2,58,87,172

Source: Balance Sheet of Channel 'A'.[1]

As can be seen from the Table, the cost of running the channel has exceeded Rs. 73 million. One of the important items in the cost relates to the production of programmes. In the case of this particular channel, cost of programmes forms more than 26 per cent of the total. The amount would have been paid as remuneration to the artists and non-artist and hire charges for securing the equipments needed to produce the programmes. News gathering forms another costly item. It accounts for about 11 per cent of the total. Production of programmes and newsgathering fall within the ambit of creative activities. They account for only 37 per cent of the total cost. The remaining portion of the cost goes to non-creative activities. Among them, telecasting cost accounted for about 26 per cent. Significantly, telecasting is the process with which the contents of the programme are transmitted to the public. Wages and salaries accounted for 14.26 per cent. Administrative costs form another category of expenditure. It accounts for about 11 per cent of the total expenditure. Table 6.2 Provides the Itemized Details of Costs and Returns of Channel B.

It could be ascertained that channel B was started with an an invested capital of Rs. 187,768,563. The total earnings of the channel came to Rs. 669,760,990 in 2005-06. On the other hand, it incurred Rs. 469,581,096 as cost on different items during that period. Thus the concern was able to make a gross profit of Rs. 200,179,894. Among the different items of cost, production expenses, in-house programmes, commissioned programmes, cost on films rights acquired etc., constitute the most important. They formed 58.02 per cent of the total cost. Most of them were meant to produce or secure cultural products of one kind or other. Compared to channel A, channel B turns out more programmes. Personal expenses which cover mainly the cost of labour incuding remuneration due to the artists accounted for 12.16 per cent of the total cost. On the other hand, the other channel spent 27 percent of the cost on this item. However, channel B does not seem to produce much of its cultural programmes directly. Instead, it gets most of such programmes produced by other agencies. What is paid to other agencies is in the form of a lumpsum payment in which labour

Table 6.2: Statement of Costs and Returns of Channel B for the Year 2005-06

A. Name of Item of Cost	*Amount Rs.*
1. Direct production expenses	272,496,267
(a) cost of in house programmes	23,815,150
(b) commissioned programmes	114,341,818
(c) news and current affairs	17,101,160
(d) cost of film right consumed	89,382,055
(e) film telecast fee	10,175,000
(f) others	6,208,934
2. Operational expenses	36,692,395
(a) transponder hire charges	34,831.140
(b) others	1,861,255
3. Personal expenses	57,111,120
(a) salary	44,934,874
(b) others	12,176,246
4. Administrative and other expenses	77,839,634
5. Interest and finance charges	25,461,680
Total (A)	469,581,096
B. Returns	
1. Sale	661,323,359
2. Other income	8,437,631
Total (B)	669,760,990
A-B	200,179,894

Source: Balance sheet of channel 'B'.[2]

cost does not figure as a separate item. Operational cost including those paid for transponder formed another major item which accounted for 7.41 per cent of the total cost. The other channel spent about 26 percent on operational cost. Being bigger in size, channel B would have been a beneficiary of economies of scale on this item. Another item is administrative cost. It also includes marketing cost. As a ratio to the total cost, administrative cost accounted for 16.7 per cent. Channel A on the other hand spent only 11 per cent on this item.

Thus huge amounts of money are spent on different items of cost. However, the bulk of the cost has gone to meet the expenses needed to cover non-creative purposes. Then the question is, what could be the motive for undertaking such business ventures calling for such high costs on various items?

Is not profit making the main consideration for undertaking such ventures? In fact, as can be seen in Table 6.2 channel B made a profit of Rs. 200,179,894 in 2005-06. In that case the question is, how channels earn profits?

As already mentioned, television is the most effective communicating system through which messages can be transmitted at multiple points. Actually, any work of art is addressed to an audience. In the absence of any easy means of communication, the messages had only a very limited size of audience in the past. With the invention of television, any messages can be relayed to an audience wider in size. Since TV is converted into a commercial activity, what the broadcaster does is producing the messages in the form of texts and communicating them as marketable commodities in the form of programmes. Certain other agencies also help the channel in the preparation and conveyance of the texts.

Programme Maker

Channels by themselves will not be able to produce all the texts and programmes apparently for various reasons. It is stated that the cost of a serial for 30 minutes duration can very well be about Rs. 1,50,000.[3] A channel may require 5-6 such serials per day in addition to the programmes like the news and various other items. The channels by themselves may not in a position to raise so much money and to produce all the texts. They may not also have sufficient expertise and man power for producing all the programmes. At the same time, as the number of channels proliferates there will be demand for more and more number of programmes. In turn, certain concerns specialising in the production of serials and programmes have emerged. The channels on their part, turn to such programme makers and purchase most of the texts from them. Channel 'B' of which we have referred earlier in Table 6.2 for instance, purchased programmes costing Rs. 114 million from such programme makers.

There has been a spurt in the number of such production units for meeting the growing demand for programmes.

According to Kohli, there are approximately 6,000 such firms in our country.[4] Balaji Telifilms, UTV Software Communications, Eros Multimedia Pvt., BAG Films and Media, Sri Adhikari Television Network, Pritish Nandy Communications, Creative Eye, Kohinoor Broadcasting Corpn., Sanguine Media, Cinevistaas, Television Eighteen, Raddaan Pictures, NTV etc., are a few leading firms with an output amounting to more than Rs. 1,000 crores in 2007-08.[5] The people associated with film world are in the fore in owning or controlling such firms. Though most of them are one man shows, some of them are well established firms. Such software firms usually sell or lease their texts to the channels. They also syndicate their texts or lease out to other channels if they are sufficiently popular. Newsgathering is another costly item for which the channels have to rely on specialized agencies to gather news originating in various places.

Cable and Satellite

Cable and satellite together form another category in the organizational arrangement of television industry. The main function of cable and satellite, as already mentioned, is to convey the contents easily and smoothly. Needless to say, conveyance is as much important as the contents of the texts. As stated earlier, there are a large number of cable operators in the field. Consumers may not be able to get access to many channels easily. Similarly, they may not be able to get connections to pay channels without installing separate set-up boxes. The consumers are able to surmount those hurdles with the help of the cable system which makes arrangements for the delivery of programmes from fifty or sixty channels at a time. Consumers can naturally select any one of the programmes from among the channels conveniently.

At the same time, a large number of satellites retransmits the programmes to the satellite dishes through their transponders. As indicated in Table 6.1 channel A for instance, spent as much as Rs. 19.1 million towards uplinking charges through satellites. At the close of the second millennium there were well over 530 satellites of all kinds over the world. Of them there were over 90 geo-stationary satellites serving the Asia-Pacific region. Among them those which engage in retransmitting programmes to India are Pan Am Sat, Insat, AsiaSat, Palapa, Apstar and so on.[6] The programmes retransmitted by the satellites in turn are distributed by the cables to the households. Since they convey the contents of different broadcasters they make the competition very effective. Thus they serve not only as conveyers of the programmes, but also as instruments in the marketing of television.

Marketing in Television

Under the capitalist mode of production, goods and services are produced for the purpose of sale. Naturally, marketing gains as much importance if not more, as that of production. Market becomes all the more important, as goods and services are produced in anticipation of demand. Since the system cannot survive without selling the goods in the market, different kinds of marketing strategies are being designed and pursued vigorously. The consumer to whom the goods are sold in the market and whose demand is crucial for the sale in the market is compared to that of a king on account his freedom of choice. Television, a unit of the culture industry, is concerned with the production of texts of varying nature which are supposed to be works of art and culture. As works of art, they are spiritual in nature and are oriented towards aesthetic qualities rather than material considerations. Apparently, they fall within the ambit of what is termed superstructure, as distinct from the economic base. Nevertheless, spiritual production also requires material resources on a limited scale mainly for meeting the mundane needs of the artists. However, texts for television call for material resources on a large scale as they are joint works of artists and non artists who make use of advanced technological instruments for the production of texts involving very high cost of production. They therefore become some sort of mercantile commodities though tinged with an artistic flavour. Naturally, norms governing the economic base come to the fore in guiding the production and telecasting of texts. Naturally, texts cannot be made and telecast as programmes without replenishing the cost. Mere replenishing the cost alone cannot be the motive for undertaking a venture involving such high cost and effort. Instead, it would be for the purpose of making gains. It calls for the marketing of television programmes. At the same time, not one channel but a plethora of channels operate in the field. As indicated in Chapter 4, there are well over 260 channels operating in our country as on 2008. Even a regional market like Kerala is flooded with more than one dozen channels. They would therefore be competing with each other for securing the maximum gain. Any work of art as already stated, is supposed to be unique in nature. However, as norms of the base acquire the upper hand, artistic standards get diluted to meet the exigencies of the market which guide the whole exercise. Accordingly, standardization and massification rule the roost for effectively meeting the competition in the market. Thus marketing which becomes crucial in the television industry also introduces new dictates in the whole exercise. Standardization acquires importance on account of another equally important marketing principle. Nobody is sure of the receptivity of a text in the market till it is actually marketed. Any feature film or tele-serial produced at high cost may turn out to be a flop in the market. Production of texts thus becomes a highly risky business as in the case of motion picture industry. Television programmes are naturally produced in the same pattern as that of motion pictures with formula films and formatting of stars, setting the standards as a safeguard against losses.

Marketing of television is beset with a number of problems for various other reasons as well. One of them relates to the nature of output in television. In the normal sense, the texts have a natural claim to be reckoned as the output in television. However, they do not serve any purpose without being telecast as programmes. Significantly, any text can be telecast again and again, if there is sufficient audience response. Apparently, they form what Throsby termed cultural capital from which income and output can flow for a long period.[7] They however, can yield an income and render any service only when they are actually conveyed to the public. Telecasting the texts, thus becomes a crucial step in the generation of output. At the same time, what is telecast must be seen and enjoyed by the audience, if at all it is to become an income generating activity. In so doing, the actual utilization becomes the key element in the generation of the output. The audience who views the programmes becomes the producer-cum-consumer of output in television as in any other service activity. Ipsofacto, what is actually utilized or experienced by the consumer alone can be treated as the output. However, the problem as indicated earlier is, how to measure the value of output as television is by and large a free service in most of the countries and anybody can view a programme with the help of an antenna. Even otherwise, it is a semi-public good which remains outside the contours of the market in the strict sense. Then a more baffling question is, how does television earn its revenue by selling its services, if it is free?

One of the usual methods adopted for the valuation of cultural goods is Contingent Valuation. It is used mainly for evaluating public goods for which the consumer does not pay any price for its use. In such cases, CV is very useful for policy purposes as for instance, the levy of a user fee. The application of such a method in the case of television may not be very helpful for many reasons. The CV of a programme cannot be collected before it is actually telecast. Availability of CV may not of much use after the telecast, as the same serial may not be repeated again. At the same time, there are many practical difficulties for collecting the CV in an authentic manner. That means the valuation of the output on the basis of CV remains an unreliable method in the case of television. Apparently, certain new norms differing from the normal marketing method would have to be adopted here. Sellers and buyers are the two players in the marketing of an ordinary commodity. Sellers represent the producers who supply the product in the market. Buyers on the other hand, purchase the products for their consumption. Television on its part renders only a cultural service. As mentioned earlier, the conveyance of the content of the text becomes equally important as that of the production of the commodity in television industry. What is conveyed should be utilized. The product will have any value only if it is conveyed and utilised. Naturally, the number of players are not limited to the two as in the case of the market in the ordinary sense. Instead, the producer of the text, also termed producer of the software, in addition to the channel or the broadcasting system, and cable networks emerge as key players from the side of supply and audience, the consumer from the side of demand. However, demand can become effective only if it is backed by sufficient purchasing power. On the other hand, the audience does not pay practically anything for viewing the programmes except perhaps the license fee wherever it is levied. What he does is, to sit in front of the TV as a viewer. That means he holds a peculiar position in the marketing of TV. Apparently, effective demand would be stemming from somebody else who is sitting behind the scene.

Ostensibly, what the channels do is to broadcast programmes, the product of the industry, and supply them at very cheap price to the audience, the consumer. Since the consumers do not pay any price channels undertake an alternative type of marketing also. It is the sale of of a portion of their service or airtime; being a part of actual broadcasting time in a day. Anybody, who is interested to convey a message of his own can do it by purchasing airtime in a channel. Businessmen avail this opportunity for broadcasting their own messages. The messages which they broadcast are advertisements meant to inform the potential buyers regarding the availability of a good or service and solicit them to purchase it. The method is akin to the practices followed by the newspapers. What the newspapers do is to sell a portion of their space in the paper and make a gain. On the other hand, channels sell a portion of their time to the advertisers, the new category of buyers. Such a practice is termed "dual product marketing" by which they "produce in two separate goods and service markets."[8] Audience to whom the regular programmes are offered forms the buyers in the first market. Advertisers who make use of the space /time to convey their own special messages form the buyers in the second market. Such dual product marketing facilitates the channels to gain substantial margin of profit even though they supply their regular commodity, the text, at very cheap price to the audience. While newspapers earn about 85 per cent of their income by selling their space to advertisers, channels earn practically the entire volume of their income from the sale of airtime. It is also beneficial to the advertisers who can directly send the message to the audience, the consumer-buyer very conveniently. Both the advertiser and audience thus form the two classes of purchasers in the television industry.

Thus, the channels on their part become some sort of brokers who link the audience and the advertiser. As in the case of brokers, the size of their income depends on the size of the audience they can deliver to the advertisers. Their marketing strategy revolves around in placating the advertiser by marshalling a large number of audience. In this process, the audience's role is being transformed into that of a dormant supplier and the advertiser's into that of an active purchaser. Apparently, some form of an equilibrating process between demand represented by the advertiser and supply represented by the audience is inherent in the whole marketing of television.

Advertiser

In the normal course, advertiser is a key player who promotes the sale in the market under the capitalist set up. What any advertisement performs is to promote the sale by informing the public regarding the availability of a product and persuading them to purchase it. Programmes in TV are also advertised by displaying the clippings and trailers of the programmes before commencing the broadcast. In fact, advertisement also forms part of the selling cost in the marketing of television as in the case of any enterprise.

Advertisement has become prominent with the industrialization and the large scale production which followed it. It has grown as a major economic activity in many countries of the world. Huge sums of money are being spent on advertisements by various business enterprises. In the US for instance, it accounted for more than 1.5 per cent of the National Product in 1998.[9] In India, the expenditure on advertisement is stated to have accounted for Rs. 20,000 crore in 2008.[10]

In order to persuade the potential buyers to purchase a particular product, they must be made aware of the special qualities of that commodity. This has to be done in the most persuasive and appealing manner, if it is to be effective. A good advertisement itself is a form of art bordering very close to magic by which audience is mesmerized about the quality of the product. Buyers are even made aware of their latent wants through effective advertisements. Advertisement has become as Williams enjoins, "the official art of modern capitalist society".[11]

Advertisement can be effective if the message reaches the maximum number of people. Media like television can reach a large number of people very conveniently. The link between television and advertisement became close because of this possibility. Ever since its inception, producers started to look upon television for the purpose of promoting the sale of their products by spending money lavishly for advertisement through TV. In the words of Barker "television is the vehicle par excellence for advertising and thus the selling of consumer goods". As he adds further "television stands at the centre of wider commercial activities and is central to the expansion of consumer capitalism".[12]

However, advertisement is not merely an activity which promotes the sale of goods but also serves as another kind of programme. In so doing, it emerges as the main source of revenue to the television channels. As indicated in Table 6.1, its contribution to the earnings of channel 'A' accounted for more than 50 per cent. In other words, it is saddled with two functions. On the one hand, it serves as an input in the sale promotion and on the other as a source of income for the channels. Thus on the one hand it is a means and on the other as an end in itself. In so doing, the advertiser emerges as the de facto purchaser of TV programmes by meeting practically the entire cost. As a matter of fact, it is the size of advertisements which forms the main source of output in TV. How it functions in such a dual capacity constitutes the peculiar aspect in the marketing of television.

When advertisement assumes the function of demand by meeting the cost of programmes, certain new developments also crop up. Any advertisement can be effective, if it can attract the attention of the people to whom it is addressed. This is done by inserting pieces of advertisements in the middle of interesting programmes. Furthermore, it should reach the maximum number of people. By utilizing TV as an advertisement medium, the advertiser aims at reaching the maximum number of people in an appealing manner. What the advertiser usually does for this purpose is to advertise through the channels which command the attention of a large number of people or the channels whose ratings are high. Evidently, prime time becomes the most sought after time for advertisements. What they usually do is, to select channels which have higher audience ratings. Channels on their part strive to catch maximum size of audience. It has therefore become a challenging task for any channel to widen the size of audience. Channels thus promote the programmes in such a way as to enhance their ratings. They may do this by taking popular issues or programmes in which people are interested. For this, they invariably dilute the artistic quality of the programmes to gain more and more of mass appeal. No wonder, sex, crime and sensational stories get undue importance in most of the programmes. Hence, the competition among the channels may revolve around stereotyped progammes such as crime stories rather than rich artistic products. Such a situation reminds of what Withers terms the application of the Principle of Minimum Differentiation.[13] Not surprisingly, most of the channels concentrate on telecasting standardized variety of tele-serials during the prime time rather than any other type of programme. Interestingly, the 7.30 P.M. news in most of the the channels have disappeared. Instead, they telecast evening news invariably at 6 P.M. or so in order to reserve the prime time for entertainment programmes.

The emergence of advertisement as a key player has in a way amounts to the revival of the patronage system in a new form. In the past, artists and writers were patronized by the rulers or the nobles. Advertisement assumes the same role in a slightly different form by patronizing the television programmes. Under the patronage system, the artists were bound to produce works according to the whims and fancies of the patron. The situation reminds one of the old proverbs 'he who pays the piper sets the tune'. Similarly, channels are very often compelled to produce programmes congenial to the interests of the advertisers. Barker expresses the same in slightly different terms; "Advertisers develop a sense of their right to have their interests served by producers and networks whose business becomes not making and transmitting programmes, but delivering audiences to the advertisers".[14] However, as in the past, the consumer public, do not pay anything for watching the programmes. They can afford to view the programmes which would have been well-nigh impossible but for the appearance of the advertiser as the patron. That means, it is the society at large which meets the cost of television programmes. In that case, the question is, should the society incur enormous sums of money on advertisements? Moreover, it is an irony that people are encouraged to consume goods which are harmful or which do not actually render any benefit at all to them. It was this issue which had invited the wrath of Frankfurt School on culture industry.

Audience

Programmes are telecast for the audience to view them. As mentioned earlier, any programme can yield an income, if at all it is utilized by the audience. Technology has advanced to such an extent that people in any part of the world can see programmes from any channel without much difficulty. However, they do not do so on account of linguistic and cultural differences. Hindi for example, is a language spoken by the majority of people in India. However, programmes in Hindi may not be welcome to people in states like Kerala, Tamil Nadu, Andhra Pradesh etc. Similarly, programmes in regional languages like Malayalam or Telugu will not have a market outside their respective linguistic boundaries. Naturally, market for any channel is limited to the size of the linguistic community. In fact, as Thomas maintains, domestic broadcasters could safeguard their audience strength from being eroded by the encroachment of transnational channels by exploiting the linguistic market.[15] In this respect, what is known as cultural discount as conceptualized by Hoskino and Mirus appears to be relevant, in so far as to uncover the extent of the market for the programmes stemming from any particular cultural or linguistic milieu. According to this concept, a programme in one language will have a diminished appeal elsewhere as viewers of one region find it difficult to identify with the language, style, values, beliefs and institutions of another region.[16] Nevertheless, programmes in world languages like English possess a wider market. Hindi in India, has also a wider market spreading across the non-Hindi speaking areas.

One of the modern developments is the presence of large number of people speaking languages other than the dominant language of the region in many parts of the world. Malaylees, the natives of Kerala for example, are found in large numbers in various other parts of India. Malayalee presence is strong not only in almost all parts of India, but also in foreign lands like the Gulf region and the US. Malayalam channels have opened their net works in the Gulf and even in the US for exploiting the markets there by catering to the needs of the expatriate Malayalees. Significantly, Channel 'B', of which we have referred in Table 6.2, earned as much as Rs. 6,63,19,655 from external marketing during the year ending 31-3-2006.[17] Similarly, Hindi channels have opened their net works in foreign lands like the Gulf region and the US. Spanish programmes could penetrate the US market apparently on account of the possibility for catering to the needs of the Hispanic people in the US. Needless to say, growth of cable and satellite could accelerate this penetration in the overseas market. Exploitation of the foreign markets is resorted to, as it is a cheap endeavour for which the programmes already created can be transmitted without incurring any extra cost.

Similarly, programmes dear to males may not have much receptivity with the females. A typical example is the programmes in sports. It is generally the male members who patronize sports programmes. Age is a factor which will also affects the receptivity of programmes. It is the youngsters in the age group 15-49 who patronise television programmes. Programmes are arranged in such a way as to cater to the needs of different categories of audiences.

The audience as indicated elsewhere, does not pay practically anything except the charges due to the cable operators and to the pay channels, as television programmes appear more or less as free goods. They are free to select any one of the programmes supplied by the cable operators. What is needed is, that they should have sufficient free time to view the programmes. Since there are large number of channels, there is a keen competition between the channels to secure the attention of maximum number of audience. Programmes which are appealing to the largest number of audience are produced or necessary ingredients are added to the programmes to catch the attention of a large size of audience. One of the techniques is to examine carefully the composition of the audience. Advertisers are interested only in audiences with sufficient purchasing power. The people who possess sufficient purchasing power in any group consist mostly of those in the age group 15-49. Naturally, programmes to catch the attention of such a group is given priority. No wonder, an author jocularly adds, "prime-time television programs are created primarily to assemble members of groups 3 and 4 for commercials".[18] Another favoured group consists of females. Soap operas are made for the purpose of attracting women audience. The timing of the programmes are also arranged in such a way as to catch the attention of various segments of the audience.

Being a cultural service in which the actual utilization rather than the content determines the output, the audience may not be able to exercise the choice for want of sufficient information. He selects a programme either on the basis of hearsay information or on the impression about the channel or the title of the programme. Audience will have to be content with what is contained in the programme. However, if he is not satisfied with a particular programme what he can do is to switch off the programme and turn to another channel.

Nature of Competition in Television Industry

Competition is the hall-mark of marketing under capitalism. Competition is supposed to ensure efficiency in production as well as high quality of the goods produced. Furthermore, the buyers become the real beneficiaries, as the goods produced are supplied at minimum possible price. In television industry, where competition is very stiff with a plethora of channels in the field, the audience can select the programmes from different channels at nominal price apparently on account of the competition among the channels.

As already stated, it is the entry of the advertiser which facilitates the supply of programmes at nil or a very nominal price to the audience by meeting practically the entire cost of the programmes from advertisements. Actually, what the broadcaster does is to ensure the presence of the audience in front of the TV and in return gets the reward in the form of advertisement charges. The channels which can assemble the largest contingent of audience gets the biggest share of the cake. Competition thus becomes a proxy war in which the audiences become mere pawns or mercenaries who boost up the power of the exhibiter.

The problem is, how to marshal a big contingent of audience and thereby to enhance the competitive strength. The channels which are affiliates of other channels or part of bigger enterprises can attract bigger size of audience. Such channels can cater to a wider market also. They may be invariably connected with advertising companies also. STAR TV for example, with such connections, is able to secure a very large contingent of audience. The track record of channels also counts much. The capacity to present appealing programmes to audience can certainly be another factor which enhances the competitive strength. Similarly, channels catering to a wider market like the national channels in India and the transnational channels like the BBC or CNN will be competitively stronger in comparison with the regional channels. However, regional channels manage to survive apparently because of the so-called cultural discount which ensures some kind of natural protection to them. Since a large number of channels are in the field, it will be difficult to draw a correct picture regarding the pulling power of any particular channel. Moreover, the audience can easily switch from one channel to another. The preference of millions of audience sitting at home and watching the programmes cannot be easily ascertained either. Apparently, it is well-neigh difficult to assess the pulling power of a channel which is termed rating in the technical jargon of the industry. At the same time, the ratings of the channels reflecting their competitive strength in the market is very essential for the channels to charge advertisers and also for the advertisers for selecting the channels for their business. It also helps the channels to plan their programmes. Naturally ratings have become an important tool in the marketing strategies of the channels.

According to the methodology adopted by the industry, the percentage of people viewing a channel as a ratio to the total number of viewers is reckoned as the basic standard for ascertaining the ratings. Different practices with most of them proving unsatisfactory, have been adopted over the years to estimate the ratings of channels. Since 2002, most of the channels in India have been following a system known as TAM (Television Audience Measurement) which is run on a 50:50 basis by two research agencies called AC Nielsen and IMRB for assessing the ratings of channels in India. Under the system, People meters installed in 6,917 homes in 148 towns and cities across India monitor the viewership pattern.[19] Whether it provides an authentic data or not, it is the main source which provides any idea on the ratings of different channels. Doordarshan also collects viewership data through sample surveys. The market share based on the ratings of different Malayalam channels prepared on the basis of TAM data as on May 2007 is as given in Table 6.3.

Table 6.3: Market Share of Different Malayalam Channels in May 2007

Sl. No.	Name of the Channel	Market Share
1.	Asianet	18.53
2.	Surya TV	18.25
3.	DD Malayalam	8.76
4.	Asianet Plus	6.0
5.	Amrita TV	4.18
6.	Kiran TV	4.07
7.	Kairali	3.37
8.	DD1	2.69
9.	Manorama News	1.62
10.	We	1.59
11.	India Vision	1.35
12.	Asianet News	1.33
13.	Jeevan	0.69
14.	People	0.4
15.	Shalom	0.4
16.	Others	26.7
	Total	100

Source: TAM Media Research Data reproduced from *A Profile Doordarshan Kendra Thiruvananthapuram*, June 2007.[20]

As can be seen from the Table, Asianet is the strongest channel closely followed by Surya TV. The competitive strength of the other channels reckoned in terms of market share is very poor compared with these two channels. Even Doordarshan with its hold on the numerically large terrestrial channel and the seemingly better quality programmes is not able to command much of the market share. Apparently, its market strategy seems to be weak to face the challenges from the satellite channels. Nevertheless, it monopolises, that part of the market where the cable has not penetrated. According to the findings of TV Viewership Survey made in 2005 by Doordarshan, Trivandrum which by and large would hold good in 2007 also, the reasons for the popularity of Surya TV were better quality, availability of new feature films, more current affairs and better coverage for news programmes.[21] Similarly, Asianet was also able to broadcast news and other quality programmes. Notwithstanding the leverage of those variables, credit should also be given to their business partnership with their affiliates in enhancing the market share.

The market share as reflected by the mere size of the audience cannot be a true indicator of the capacity of a channel to command more revenue. The size of the audience at the prime time and the composition of the audience on the basis of their age, sex, educational background and socio-economic profile are more important factors in attracting advertisers to the channels. Actually as Page and Crawley maintain "Television channels operate on the 80; 20 principle, where 80 per cent of the programmes earn 20 per cent of the revenue and the top 20 per cent of the programmes earn 80 per cent of the revenues."[22] The reason seems to be that advertisers are interested in the programmes which attract economically active audience who has the means to purchase the goods advertised in the TV and not the overall size of audience. In the opinion of Bignell both the advertisers and broadcasters believe alike that the audience composed of such people will purchase the goods advertised "during the time that they are not watching the television".[23] Channels naturally concentrate in making prime time programmes as appealing as possible. The usual methods are, as mentioned earlier, formatting of stars, adoption of formulas which have proved successful, introduction of sensational stories etc. The strategy is somewhat similar to that of what is adopted in film industry. In order to improve their ratings in the market, the channels on their part look at the rating of each programme and inject suitable ingredients to the theme or format. Each channel evolve suitable strategies in such a way as to attract more number of viewers.

Notwithstanding the adoption of TAM as the basis of ascertaining the pulling power of each channel, it is not free from defects. The people meter installed in the houses is supposed to pick up the data as to who is watching a programme from which channel at a given moment of time. A sample covering around 7,000 households cannot represent the universe in a vast country like India. People meters are installed only in the cities with a population of more than one lakh. Apparently, more than half the number of households are left out of the purview. Furthermore, certain states like Bihar and those from North east are not covered by TAM.[24]

Business Practices

Being motivated by the urge for making profit various business practices designed to maximize profit have been evolved. The arrangements of the programme is one among them. Programme time is divided into prime time and non prime time. Viewership will be intense during prime time which is normally from about 6-10 P.M. everyday. Programmes which can attract bigger size of audience are scheduled during this period of time. Even the duration of most of the programmes is fixed for 30 minutes each. It is designed to plan advertisements in a systematic manner. Nevertheless, longer duration is provided for telecasting feature films and sport programmes.

Another practice relates to the manner in which texts which are not produced by the channel are acquired and telecast. One method is the outright purchase of texts. Channels purchase satellite right of films which have made hit in the market. They also purchase serials and other programmes. Certainly it is a costly business. STAR TV was stated to be paying anywhere between Rs. 1,00,000-3,00,000 for a soap episode of 30 minutes a few years back. After the purchase, what they used to do has been to package the programme with advertisements in their own networks. Such a practice is termed promos.[25] Another method is, to lease out air time to the producers. Under the scheme the programme will be owned by the producer. Leasing out is normally fixed for a duration of 30 to 60 minutes. The producer should undertake to give a minimum guarantee depending on the time slot and expected earnings from advertisements. Rates vary from channel to channel and from day to day. Doordarshan has divided channels into national and regional categories and different rates are fixed for the various categories of channels. Even the rates may vary from day to day and from hour to hour. DD's charge for sponsored programme of 30 minutes duration was Rs. 1,25,000 in 1994. Sponsorship fee was Rs. 2,40,000 on Sundays. A Hindi feature film carried a sponsorship fee of Rs. 6,50,000.[26] Doordarshan Kendra Trivandrum has been charging sponsorship fee of Rs. 70,000 on Saturdays and Rs. 1,00,000 on Sundays since 2007 for feature films. Sponsorship also varied from Rs. 3,500 in the case of cookery shows to Rs. 70,000 for Malayalam film songs.[27] Sun TV charges sponsorship fee within the range of Rs. 100,000 to Rs. 145,000.[28]

Perhaps the most important aspect of the business practice relates to the selling of time for advertisement inclusive of Free Commercial Time (FCT) to the sponsor. The sponsor, who leases air time actually operates as an intermediary in a chain of business transactions. Invariably, he is the producer of the programmes who leases airtime for making a gain. The sponsor is usually provided with 90 seconds FCT for advertisement and two credit lines both of which he could sell for making an income. He is able to make any gain by selling his FCT for other advertisements. Advertiser thus becomes the final purchaser of air time by spending money on advertisements in the midst of programmes. The international standard is to allot 5 minutes time for advertisement for every 30 minutes programme. The Indian practice is not to limit to such a time frame and here advertisement time may be stretched upto 10-15 minutes for exceptionally popular programmes.[29] The rates will be very high during the prime time as the size of audience will be very large during this time. The rates will be low during non-prime time. In the case of TV, time lost is lost for ever. Naturally the guiding principle is to fill the time by lowering the rates during non-prime time. The system of lowering the tariff by TV during non-prime time is somewhat similar to what hotels or airlines do in such a situation. If the room remains unoccupied, the hotels do not get any income at all. During the slack season, hotels therefore charge a low rate. Similarly, airlines charge lower rate during slack season. Channels also follow the same pattern and charge a low rate during non prime time. Whatever income the channel gets, is a net gain for it.

The channels also charge spot rates for advertisements. Spot rates of advertisement varied from Rs. 15,000-70,000 with DD 1 in 2006.[30] Zee TV's rate varies from Rs. 75,000 for peak hours for 10 seconds to Rs. 60,000 for 10 seconds for non peak time.[31] Spot buying rate of Sun TV during peak hours has been Rs. 14,000 for 10 seconds since 2006. Reduced rates are being charged at non prime-time.[32] Doordarshan Kendra Trivandrum charges Rs. 12,000 as spot rate during evenings on Saturdays and Sundays. On other days, the rate varies within the range of Rs. 2,000 to 9,000 depending on the time.[33] Most of the channels give certain incentives and bonuses to the advertisers.

Most of the transactions relating to advertisements are being arranged through advertising agencies, another class of stakeholders in the marketing of television. Packages of advertisements for a period of three months at concessional rates are also offered by the channels for the purpose of ensuring the regular supply of advertisements. These agencies seem to have acquired so much importance as to reduce the rates or even to cancel the advertisements, if the ratings fall.

Sources of Income

The most important marketing practice is to lease the programme time or to sell the air time to use the technical language of the industry. The purchaser becomes the sponsor of the programmes and he pays a fixed amount to the channel. What the channel gets from the sponsorship forms the important source of income. The channel on its part as mentioned earlier, allots a few seconds, termed FCT to the sponsor. In addition, the channel sells slots of time on a spot sale basis. Such sales are made to the advertisers who do not sponsor the programmes. Another source is the earnings from the sale on sundry items. Thus advertisement charges of one kind or other form the main source of earnings of the channels.

Notwithstanding the emergence of advertisement as some sort of monopsonist in purchasing the programmes en masse, audience also shed out money in certain cases for seeing the programmes. In those countries like Great Britain for example, where public system of broadcasting is still in existence, the owners of TV sets are bound to pay a license fee of 131 pounds a year, whether they see any programme or not.[34] As mentioned earlier, license fee has been totally abolished in India though remnants of public system of broadcasting is still in vogue.

The public also share a portion of the price by way of paying the subsçription to cable TV. Though most of the programmes are free, the public have to pay a subscription charge for the cable which deliver programmes of many channels. The cost which they pay is mainly for meeting the investment cost and operational cost of the cable operators. There are also some channels whose programmmes can be viewed by the audience against the payment of a subscription fee. Such channels are known as pay channels. The charge seems to be around Rs. five per channel. Most of the channels conduct their business through the cable operators. The channels share the receipts with the cable operators. There are well over 110 pay channels in India.[35] Some of them are directly connected to the audience through a set-top-box to receive and decrypt the signal.

Earnings of Different Channels in India

The size of a channel's earnings depends on various factors. As already stated, the ratings both of the channel and of its programmes are of crucial importance in determining the size of its earnings. However, Crawley and William maintain that the channels rather than the programmes are far more important. Channels which have made a name in the market are in a position to attract more advertisement revenues. In their words, "Zee's ability to capture advertisements for its mass entertainment channel is not because Zee's programmes are necessarily better but because for most people in northern, central and western India it is the channel they switch to first".[36] Another important factor is the extent of the market into which a channel caters its products. The texts, the products of the channel, are produced in a language spoken by the audience. People speaking one languages may not normally watch the programmes in other languages because of the so called cultural discount. The people speaking a particular language constitute the market for the programmes in that language. Apparently, numerically larger languages will have bigger markets. Similarly, channels connected with networks or affiliated to other channels will be able to earn larger volume of income.

Some of the Indian private channels manage to earn fairly large volume of income by selling their services during recent years. According to the estimates prepared by CMIE (Centre for Monitoring Indian Economy) leading private Indian channels in India, could earn Rs. 3,607.30 crore in 2007-08. These channels were able to earn only Rs. 906.37 crore in 2002-03.[37] There was thus, a four-fold increase in the size of their earnings within a period of six years.

Table 6.4 gives the amount of earnings made by the important Indian private channels from sales during 2002-03 and 2007-08.

Table 6.4: Earnings of Important Indian Private Channels

	Name of the Channel	*Earnings 2002-03*	*Earnings 2007-08 (Rs. Crores)*
1.	Zee Entertainment Enterprises	470.59	1041.73
2.	Sun TV Networks	221.10	861.06
3.	Zee News	0	358.22
4.	New Delhi Television	103.03	304.93
5.	Television Eighteen India	0	287.50
6.	TV Today Network	108.48	230.91
7.	Sahara One Media & Entertainment	54.79	197.25
8.	Ibn 18 Broadcast	0	131.18
9.	Raj Television Network	30.17	57.13
10.	NDTV Media	0.05	43.10
11.	Malayalam Communications	11.32	25.37
12.	Jain Studios	2,27	21.93
	Others	11.31	46.99
	Total	906.37	3607.30

Source: CMIE April 2009; *Industry, Market Size and Shares*; p. 406.
(Others consist of: Times Global Broadcasting Co, Broadcast Worldwide, and Astha Broadcasting Network)

As can be seen in the Table, the channels were able to earn fairly good amount of income from the sale of their services within a short period of their openings. With a wide market in the Hindi heartland, Zee which transmits most of its programmes in Hindi, tops the list. A few channels in regional languages like Punjabi, Gujarati and some specialized channels like Zee music are also affiliated to Zee. NDTV, an English channel with an all India market is not able to come anywhere near Zee apparently on account of linguistic barrier. However, Sun a regional channel with programmes mainly in Tamil comes second. Some channels in other south Indian languages and also those with specialized programmes are also affiliated to Sun. Regional channels like Malayalam Communications or Raj are also able to make a niche in the market by properly catering to the linguistic audience. All these channels telecast programmes to the diasporic Indians settled in various foreign countries also. Significantly, some of the channels opened since 2002-03 like Television Eighteen or Ibn networks could also earn fairly good amount of income. The list does not cover all the hundred and odd channels telecasting in India. Most of them like Asianet, Enadu, JJ TV, Indiavision and so on would also be earning fairly large volume of income from the market.

Conclusion

Marketing of TV with its cultural products for sale is a complicated affair for various reasons. The product mix generates any amount of value as and when it is actually utilized by the consumer. However, the usual parameter for measuring the value of the product mix on the basis of actual utilization becomes meaningless as it is invariably offered as a free good. Channels compensate the loss of revenue arising from the free supply of programmes by selling the airtime to the advertisers. What transpires in such a dual product marketing amounts to the functioning of the audience as supplier and the advertiser as the purchaser. The strategies and practices of this type of marketing are evolved in such a way as to equilibrate the audience-advertiser interaction. Most of the Indian channels earn a substantial volume of income by adopting the marketing of their products on similar lines.

NOTES AND REFERENCES

1. Data collected from the balance sheet of a private channel called A.
2. Data collected from the balance sheet of channel B.
3. Anitha, Kohli (2003). *The Indian Media Business*, New Delhi, Response Books, p. 84.
4. Anitha, Kohli (2003). *op. cit.*, p. 83.
5. CMIE (Centre for Monitoring Indian Economy) (April 2009). *Industry: Market Size and Shares Media Content*, p. 408.
6. Thomas Amos Owen (2005). *Imagi-Nations and Borderless Television*, Sage, pp. 40-51.
7. Throsby, David (2001). *Economics and Culture*, Cambridge, University Press, pp. 45-50.
8. Albarran, Alan B. (2003). *Media Economics; Understanding Markets Industries and Concepts*, New Delhi, Surjeet Publications, p. 27.
9. Hesmondhalgh, David (2002). *The Cultural Industries*, New Delhi, Sage Publications, p. 91.
10. www.television point.com/news 2009.
11. Williams, Raymond (1993). "Advertising: The Magic System" in Simon During (ed.); *Cultural Studies*, London, Routledge, p. 334.
12. Barker, Chris (1997). *Global Television*, Oxford, Blackwell Publishers, p. 21.
13. Withers, Glenn (2003). "Broadcasting" in Ruth Towse (ed.); *A Handbok of Cultural Economics*, Cheltenham Edward Elgar, p. 107.
14. Barker, Chris (1997). *op. cit.*, p. 156.
15. Thomas Amos Owen (2005). *op. cit.*, New Delhi, Sage Publications, p. 21.
16. Barker, Chris (1997). *Global Television*, Oxford Blackwell Publishers, p. 50.
17. Balance sheet of channel B.
18. Marc, David (1984). *Demographic Vistas; Television in American Culture*, University of Pennsylvania Press, p. 14. According to him those in the age group 18-34 form category 3 and 35-55 form category 4.
19. CMS (Centre for Media Studies) (2007). *Television Vierwership and Measurement: Dilemma and Challenges*, New Delhi, p. 19.
20. Doordarshan Kendra Thiruvananthapuram, A Profile June 2007.
21. TV Viewers Survey Thiruvanathapuram Jan, 2005 (Audience Research Unit, Doordarshan Kendra, Thiruvananthapuram).
22. David, Page and William, Crawley (2001). *Satellites Over South Asia; Broadcasting Culture and Public Interest*, New Delhi, Sage Publications, p. 122.
23. Jonathan, Bignell (2004). *An Introduction to Television Studies*, London, Routledge, p. 255.
24. CMS (2007). *op. cit.*

25. Kohli, Anitha (2003). *op. cit.*, p. 79.
26. Bhatt, S.C. (1994). *Satellite Invasion of India*, New Delhi, Gyan Publishing House, pp. 253-75.
27. Doordarshan Kendra Tvm Rate Cards as on 1-4-2007.
28. www.indiatelevision.com/headlines for the rates of SUN TV.
29. Kohli, Anitha (2003). *op. cit.*, p. 89.
30. www.ddindia,gov.in/Business/Commercial+And +Sales dt 11/24/ 2007.
31. www.televisionpoint.com/news 2006 for Zee TV Rates.
32. Prasar Bharati Doordarshankendra Thiruvananthapuram *op. cit.*
33. see www.indiantelevision.com/headlines for the rates of SUN TV.
34. *The Economist*, 6 June 2007.
35. www.saveondish.com/110-pay-channels.
36. Page and William Crawley (2001). *op. cit.*, p. 128.
37. CMIE (2009). *op. cit.*, p. 406.

7

Artistic Labour Market in the Television Industry

Remuneration to labour is perhaps the most baffling problem in economics. Scholars have evolved different theories on this problem on different occasions with none of them providing a satisfactory explanation. Very often, payment is made on an adhoc basis or on the basis of rule of the thumb. The question becomes all the more complicated in the case of reward to the artists. "Artistic labour markets" as Throsby enjoins "present some intriguing challenges to a labour economist seeking to understand the standard variables usually considered in models of labour market behaviour-labour supply, wage determination, earnings, distributions, career paths and so on."[1] Unlike the ordinary labour, artists are not solely guided by monetary gains. In fact, in the good old days, art was regarded as a collective activity for which the society as a whole or public authority assumed the responsibility for paying remuneration.

Things have changed with the entry of market as the arbiter in paying remuneration to artists. Under the new dispensation, the mentality to look upon artists within the category of labour has gained ascendancy. Nevertheless, remuneration is being paid to the artist not as a mere labourer but as a different category of worker. The emergence of culture industry with its tentacles spread into many branches of art, has added new dimensions to the art labour market. Needless to say, the situation remains fluid with different practices and yardsticks.

Different Kinds of Labour in the Culture Industry

Before proceeding further into this question, a word of explanation would be required regarding the different kinds of labour which man the culture industry, particularly in relation to television. They can be divided broadly into technical, administrative-cum-managerial and artists.

Any industry calls for the services of different categories of labour. However, most of the industries of the modern period rely on technical labour. Technical labour in television ranges from the highly advanced sound engineers to the ordinary technical hands. The cameraman, the editing staff, the processing staff, floor manager etc., also fall within the category of technical personnel. Though their services are required in all stages of production, they are the key players in the reproduction and circulation of the products which are also termed texts.

Since productive units are organized on factory line with large number of people in their roll, different kinds of activities have to be managed. The goods are produced for selling or for catering to the needs of the audience for getting a profit. Efficient management and marketing would be required as a crucial determinant for those purposes. On account of the complex nature of television industry, the latest practice is to call the personnel of such a category as professional labour. They, according to an author, form some sort of a new kind of priesthood mediating between events and audiences and also between artists and technicians.[2] They are also termed creative managers as the management of the cultural enterprises are undertaken by them.[3] In addition, the services of accountants, typists and other categories of ordinary labour are also needed in television industry.

Artistic Labour

What a culture industry like television does is to create texts of different kinds for circulation. They are rooted in culture carrying symbolic meaning. Since the texts carry symbolic meaning, artists are also known as symbol creators. It is the artists who conceive the idea of such products and create them. Ordinary labour is not in a position to turn out such creative products.

Inevitably, a distinction between artists and ordinary labour becomes apparent. As mentioned earlier, Kant regarded ordinary labor as mercenary labour and artist as free labour. Such a distinction is drawn because ordinary labour performs work under compulsion. Artists on the other hand, undertake artistic work for getting a pleasure by creating a work or for getting recognition. Though they require material resources they undertake artistic creation not for monetary reward as such. Because of such differences artistic activities remain autonomous. Even Marxists, who do not regard artists as a separate category of workers, are prepared to concede the importance of artists in creating works of art. In a branch of culture industry like television, artists are treated as a separate class of workers and accordingly certain amount of autonomy, not usually granted to other kinds of workers, is bestowed on them.

The texts which television turns out are created as a combined work of different kinds of workers. Since, artists conceive the idea of the products in television, they form the most important class among the workers. Nevertheless, artists and cultural workers also constitute a heterogeneous class. The services of performing artists, in the form of histrionic services form the most important input in the production of the texts in television. The important categories of cultural products of television as mentioned in Ch 5 consists of tele-serials, film based programmes, drama etc. Musicians, dancers, directors, script writers, make up men, costume makers etc., also come in the picture by rendering their services containing artistic ingredients. Writers of news or so to say, journalists and commentators of programmes and even cameramen also require artistic skills. They also fall within the category of artists in a broader sense too.

Conditions of Service

Being a branch of culture industry, production in television would be carried on under an assembly line as in a factory. However, most of the acting and shooting are undertaken in localities away from the factories or the studios. At the same time, the artists of the television industry do not work as regular factory hands. Instead, they work invarably, as freelance artists. They work so to say, on contracts for short periods. As Throsby enjoins, "most of the performing artists, even though formally speaking they are employees, are likely to work on a sporadic or short term contract basis."[4] They therefore are in a position to retain their independence and autonomy. Many of them work overtime without taking into acçount financial considerations. As Francoise notes hard training, low rate of success stories, risky careers and short term contracts seem to be inherent to artistic choices.[5] Since artistic performances are carried on invariably as a part-time activity most of the artists may take up employment in other occupations apparently for meeting their mundane needs. In other words, multiple job-holding has become a regular phenomenon in the case of artists as a whole.

Under the modern conditions, the artists are not able to engage in creative work without the backing of organizational support. As Hesmondhalgh notes, "All creators have an audience, and in the modern world no one can do this without the help of technological mediation and the support of large organizations".[6] To that extent, their independence becomes weak. Many of them, as he adds further, "are forced to do creative work that they hardly experience as creative at all". No wonder, most of them acquire commercial motives and an inclination to work for money.

Remuneration to the Artists

Mainstream economics regards wages as a price-the price for the service of labour. Accordingly, wages are determined by the interaction of demand for and supply of labour. Demand for labour arises for the value of the product rendered by the labourer and wages are paid on the basis of marginal productivity. However, in the case of a product of the culture industry, value remains elusive and indeterminate. Naturally, measurement of value has to be made on an adhoc basis or as Heilburn enjoins "on indirect measures or proxies."[7] As he adds further, it makes the worth of an individual performer very difficult to ascertain.[8] Apparently, the marginal revenue product which forms the basis of price for labour and the volume of employment cannot be known in the case of a branch of culture industry like television. At the same time, productivity per se, does not improve with technological progress in the case of artists as in the case of ordinary labour. Inevitably, conventional theories become somewhat meaningless with regards to creative workers or artists of culture industry. Accordingly, artistic remuneration is being paid on the basis of special norms.

As a matter of fact, a number of practices have evolved over the years in respect of the payment of remuneration to artists. One of them is to make remuneration on the basis of royalty. Under royalty, a percentage of the total earnings or profit is paid to them. The percentage varies from 10 to 20 per cent of the output depending on the popularity of the artists. Most of the countries have made laws fixing the rate and conditions of payment of royalty. Royalty is applicable mainly for authors or musicians. Apparently, royalty does not figure on any significant scale as a yardstick in the case of television.

Instead, in television industry, as also with any other branch of culture industry, remuneration is paid mainly on the basis of contract. However, it is reported that majority of the artists in the West are paid very low amount of remuneration and accordingly artists are very often termed a starving class. One reason for the low rate is the oversupply of artists. If so, the question is, why do so many youngsters flock to the art market. The willingness of artists to work for low wages in anticipation of getting recognition seems to be one reason for this anomalous situation. Furthermore, artistic activities are supposed to bring glamour and recognition also. However, many of them fail to get recognition and in turn entry into these fields, as an author puts, has many aspects of a lottery in which only a few obtain the big prizes (9). While many entrants turn to other less risky ventures in course of time, those who are endowed with artistic skills alone cling to artistic works. An equally valid reason is the theory of art for arts sake. According to the theory, artists are prepared to create works of art for the mental satisfaction they get from this.

However, artists in the television industry in India are not so poorly paid. According to the industrial sources, ordinary serial actors in a regional channel like that of Malayalam are getting lucrative salaries in between Rs. 3,000 and Rs. 15,000 per programme of about half an hour duration. Nevertheless, reputed artists get around Rs. 50,000 for a similar programme. Stars in Tamil or Hindi may get even upto ten times higher than that of Malayalam stars, depending on their stature.[10] We are not in a position to state whether there is an oversupply of artists. However, many youngsters enter into the field for serial acting even for a meagre sum at Rs. 1,000 as remuneration per episode, apparently in anticipation of getting recognition at a later date. However, many of them are exploited and cheated. A good number of female artists who are lured with promises to act in television, becomes victims to sexual exploitation also.

Another distressing aspect relates to the wide variations in the quantum of remuneration to different classes of artists in the culture industry. Among the performing artists, the superstars get disproportionately high rate of remuneration. The system of paying very high rate of remuneration to super stars stems from what is known as formatting of stars which has emerged as a prudent business strategy in film industry. The system was introduced for ensuring good collections in the box office to films which face a totally uncertain demand in the market till they are actually exhibited. Accordingly, as Vogel enjoins "It may be less risky to pay a star $1.5 million than to pay an unknown $1,00,000; the presence of the star may easily increase the value of property by several times that $1.5 million salary through increased sales in theatrical and other markets, whereas the unknown may contribute nothing from the standpoint of return on investment."[11] Furthermore, audiences prefer the programmes performed by such superstars who dominate the scene on account of their superior talents. In turn, such stars who cannot be easily substituted command very high rate of remuneration. Presumably, differences in talent which can be reckoned as a form of rent count much in such payments. Human capital has also a role in the picture.

Taking a different stand authors like, Rosen contend that the widening of the demand arising with the growth of culture industry operates as the crucial factor in the emergence of superstars. In his opinion "if demand for services is sufficiently elastic—rents of sellers increase and in turn there is greater concentration in the distribution of rewards among the most talented".[12] The emergence of culture industry has reduced the real price of entertainment services, but has enlarged the scope of each performer's audience. Inevitably, superstars are able to command very high amount of remuneration.

The element of super star is not confined to films or TV alone. It is also widespread in sports and various other fields thanks to the influence of television. As Rosen enjoins, television has had an enormous impact on the income of top bowlers, golfers and tennis players because their markets have expanded.[13] Sachin Tendulakar for example, earns approximately $14 million annually, apparently because of the wider demand created by TV.[14]

However, Rosen's reasons do not seem to be relevant to explain the wide variations in the volume of remuneration commanded by the super stars belonging to different linguistic films. It is stated that the superstars in Hindi like Amitabh Bachchan could command as high as Rs. one crore as remuneration during 1980s or Shah Rukh Khan commands Rs. seven crore, Aamir Khan Rs. five to six crore, Salman Khan Rs. five and half crore or Hrithik Roshan Rs. five crore and so on. Interestingly, female stars get lower rate of remuneration compared to the males. Among the females Kareena Kapoor is stated to be getting Rs. 2.25 crore, perhaps the highest for a female star.[15] Similarly, none of the superstars in Malayalam earns anywhere near that figure. Their maximum range is in between Rs. 7.5 million to 12.5 million.[16] Super stars in Tamil or Telugu get remuneration much higher than that of Malayalam stars.[16] Interestingly, it is reported that Rajani Kanth, the leading super star in Tamil could surpass the Hindi super stars and top the list by commanding as high as Rs. 16 crores as remuneration. Such wide variations could be attributed primarily to the size as well as special characteristics of the linguistic market arising from the cultural discount per se, which as we have seen creates a niche in the market for the texts of each language, than to the widening of the audience effected by television. However, as the original and indestructible fertility of the land fetches higher and higher amount of rent with every extension of cultivation, the super stars of large linguistic markets command higher rates of remuneration for their unique qualities which cannot be substituted.

The stars in television do not command as high a reward as the film stars apparently on account of the competition among the large number of artists. As a matter of fact, super stars do not normally take up acting in television programmes. Serials which form the most important cultural product of televisions run for months with one episode for each day. In turn, production becomes a continuous process as broadcast continues. The superstars with heavy schedules do not have the inclination or the time to act in such serials. Furthermore, they may not be able to retain their hold by acting in the serials which run for months. On the other hand, most of the stars next below the super stars appear in tele-serials without any hesitation. However, the retired stars and junior stars are those who dominate the mini-screen. Needless to say, the young artists who appear in television look upon television as a stepping stone for their career into the films, later perhaps.

The glamour industry like television does not seem to be transparent in its financial dealings, particularly relating to the remuneration to the artists. Clock of secrecy and clandestine dealings seem to be widespread. Producers and the stars alike are reluctant to divulge the actual volume of money paid or received. Secrecy is maintained as one of the strategies for meeting the competition from other channels effectively. An equally important reason seems to be the inclination to avoid the payment of tax. Furthermore, black money seems to be active in the whole affair. Such a legacy seems to have been inherited from film industry. Film industry provides ample scope for the involvement of black payments at different stages of production. Film producers can inflate the figures without bringing the facts to the attention of tax collecting authorities and get back purified money by way of traveling allowance and remuneration to the artists in excess of the sum contracted for.[17] Such a scenario seems to be prevalent in television also. Indeed, a good number of the producers seems to rely on television industry as a fertile field for black money transactions. Instead of collecting fixed salary, some of the stars earn their share by becoming partners in the production of films. Some of the channel authorities or operatives, whom we met were reluctant even to disclose the rates of advertisement charges levied by them, let alone the rate of remuneration to the artists.

Conclusion

Labour market pertaining to television industry operates under altogether different conditions from that of other industries. Supply of artists is far beyond the requirements. Naturally, the workers are underemployed and also under paid. They are contented with low wages apparently because of the glamour attached to cultural industry like television. There is wide variations in the actual amount of remuneration paid to the artists as a class with the superstars earning abnormally high rate of remuneration. However, serial actors do not command very high rate of remuneration compared to film stars.

NOTES AND REFERENCES

1. Throsby, David (001). *Economics and Culture,* Cambridge, University Press, p. 120.
2. Smith, Anthony (1998). "Introduction" in Anthony Smith (ed.) *Television: An International History,* Oxford University Press, p. 6.

3. David, Hesmondhalgh (2002). *Cultural Industries,* London, Sage Publications, p. 53.
4. Throsby. *op. cit.,* p. 120.
5. Benhamou Francoise (2003). "Artist's Labour Markets" in Towse Ruth (ed.) *A Handbook of Cultural Economics,* Cheltenham, Edward Elgar, p. 71.
6. Hesmondhalgh. *op. cit.,* p. 71.
7. Heilburn, James and Grey Charles M. (2001). *Economics of Art and Culture,* Cambridge University Press, p. 108.
8. Heilburn *et al.* (2001). *op. cit.,* p. 327.
9. Rosen Sherwin (1986). "The Theory of Equalising Differences" in. Ashenfelter and Richard Layard (eds.) *Handbook of Labour Economics* Vol. 1, Amsterdam, North Holland, p. 681.
10. Interview with Sri P. Mohanan.
11. Vogel Harold, L. (2004), *Entertainment Industry Economics: A Guide for Financial Analysis,* Oxford University Press, p. 133.
12. Sherwin, Rosen (1981). "The Economics of Superstars" in *The American Economic Review,* Vol. 71, No. 5.
13. Sherwin, Rosen (1981). *op. cit.*
14. *The Hindu,* 16th December, 2007.
15. http://desitrain.com/2006 Bollywood Salaries.
16. Bijoy, A.K. (2005). "Films Become Hot Property for Malayalam Channels" in Indian Television.com.
17. Oommen and Joseph (1991). *Economics of Indian Clnema,* Delhi, Oxford and IBH Publishing Company, pp. 125-26.

8

Audience Response to Television Programmes

An Empirical Analysis

In the previous chapter, we have seen how the audience appears in the picture as a player in the market. Programmes are prepared and telecast for the enjoyment of the audience. In a sense, the utilization of the programmes by the audience constitutes the volume of output in television industry. They should therefore be actively responding to the programmes.

Position of Audience in the Television Industry

Audience are perhaps the most sought after class of people in the television industry. They are sought not on account of the size of their purse. As already stated in the earlier chapter, they do not pay practically anything for viewing the programmes. They are sought after because their appearance in front of the TV as reflected in the rating is the main consideration for getting large volume of revenue from the advertisers. Apparently they must be very powerful players in the television industry.

On the other hand, authors like Lodziak are of the opinion that the audience holds only a weak position in television industry. As he puts it "the highest television viewing groups tend to be found amongst the least powerful and it is the relative powerlessness of these groups which may provide a powerful reason for their high viewing". He maintains that they tend to view television because of the absence of alternative occupations.[1] Evidently, they would not contemplate to view television if they are gainfully occupied in other activities. Though his contention as such may not hold good under all circumstances, the transmission of the programmes within a strict time schedule makes the position of the audience somewhat weak. He has to see the programmes as and when it appears in the channel. However with the technological improvements, he can store the programme in CD and view them when he is free. The alternative before him is to switch off and turn to another channel. The programmes in other channels may also not be agreeable to his taste.

The quality of any programme can be known only after actually seeing it. At the same time, any programme is a flow which is neither stored as in the case of a book, nor repeated as in the case of motion pictures under normal circumstances. Furthermore, if the viewer is not selecting the programme within the time schedule, the time available for him also will be lost and he cannot store the time. Because of these peculiar conditions under which audience have to operate, coupled with the need for the physical presence of the audience in front of the TV, the broadcasters as Hartley maintains, are in a position to approach the audience as children. The broadcasters as he puts, "appeal to the playful, imaginative, fantacy, irresponsible aspects of adult behaviour—What better, then, than a fictional version of every body's supposed childlike tendencies which might be understood as predating such social groupings"[2] Bignell who toes to the same line of thinking regards the approach as a strategy of control. In his words," it is based on the basic assumption that television viewers seeking pleasure and entertainment, unconsciously wish to regress to a childlike state".[3] In consonance to such an approach children's programmes and even other programmes are tuned in such a way as parents address children. Such a strategy is adopted by each channel for the explicit purpose of attracting as big an audience as possible and to retain their preference to that channel with an eye on the flow of the earnings from advertisements. In such a situation, the audience may be even regarded as a mercantile commodity offered to to the consumption of the advertiser.[4]

Instead of treating the audience as children, a better analogy would perhaps be to compare the position of the audiences to that of the mercenaries who boost the combat strength of the monarchs and rulers. Those who possess a numerically big army are in a position to bargain in any trial of strength and can collect a better share of the booty or royalty. Somewhat similar to what the rulers do in providing food and other incentives to the mercenaries, the broadcasters entertain the audience with free supply of programmes and other attractions to keep them in good humour. As the rulers are keen to have a large army comprising the youngsters, the broadcasters are interested in attracting an audience with high purchasing power and not with the overall size of the audience.

The broadcasters manipulate the childlike qualities of the audience in order to boost the ratings of the progammes which is the main criterion for attracting a large share of revenue from the advertisers. The audiences who are hooked up to the programmes or the text remain as mere passive audiences. They blindly accept what the texts convey as genuine like the children of Hamelin who followed the Piper. In such cases the meaning which the audience draws is invariably determined by the texts themselves. On the other hand, audiences may also become active by deriving meanings of their own from the texts. Actually all texts are polysemics, capable of providing multiple meanings. In other words, most of the texts carry multiple meanings which can be interpreted in different ways. In the words of Barker, text contains "indeterminacy and gaps whereby the reader moves through the texts and engages in a process of gap filling and meaning construction by which expectations are modified in a dynamic process of interaction between the readers anticipation and the texts of the schematic instructions and invitations".[5] In such cases, audiences make or take meanings of their own which may be different from what the maker of the texts intended.[6] If so, audiences may turn out to be an elusive class who cannot be easily convinced. It will be also very difficult to control and regulate their attitude and behaviour.[7]

Audience may also become active in selecting programmes

of their own. Such freedom of choice stems mainly on account of the competition among the channels. In selecting the programmes they tend to carry with them their own identity and evince an interest to see the programmes which are agreeable to their own culture. It is this cultural leaning of the audience which accounts for the limitation of market to the size of linguistic entities. The regional channels in turn as stated in the previous Chapter, are able to withstand the competition from the transnational channels by taking advantage of the pulling power of the identity of audience with the supply of programmes rooted in the regional culture.

Any channel, on its part transmits a wide variety of programmes round the clock every day. Apparently, a person cannot see all the programmes. He can spend only a few hours in front of the TV for viewing the programmes on any day. The time he is able spare in front of the TV is conditioned by his daily routine. He can find time for viewing TV only after allotting time for what is known as the realm of necessity comprising pledge time, that is paid labour time, compulsive time, meaning time required for domestic activities, and personal time denoting time for sleeping, eating etc.[8] The time available after meeting the realm of necessity is termed free time or leisure time which he can utilize as he likes. The quantum of free time available, and the extent thereof utilized for viewing TV varies from person to person depending his calling in life, stage of life cycle, educational qualification, sex, socio-economic status, etc. It also varies from country to country. Apparently, in most of the less developed countries, the leisure time at the disposal of the bulk of the population will be for short duration. However, the data pertaining to the response of the audience in relation to the duration of viewing time are totally nil for practical purposes in countries like India. Similarly, the programmes selected and watched by the audience are also unknown variables as the audience is not a homogenous group.

What the programmes convey is the culture in its various manifestations from different places. They contain a wide variety of cultural messages. Many of them will be absorbed or assimilated in course of time by the audience as part of their own culture. Thus they become part and parcel of the culture of the audience. In so doing, TV becomes a powerful diffusing agent. However, as Shanhan and Morgan pointed out "the culture level effect is much more difficult to gauge in the same sense that it is difficult to measure the impact of the air in our breathing."[9] Nevertheless, it may be possible to assess the contours of the impact to some extent by gathering the information from the horses own mouth through a field study.

Furthermore, knowledge on various fields and the skill formation of the audience also get improved by watching TV programmes. Similarly, changes also take place in the habits and material conditions of life of the audiences by frequently exposing to TV. They may demand new kinds of goods by seeing the advertisements in the TV. The extent of such changes is also an unknown factor. In sum, the behavioural pattern of the people towards TV, their viewing habits, attitude towards different varieties of programmes, the impact which TV exerts and so on are imponderable factors.

Field Study in Kerala

In view of the complex nature of the response of the audience and its wider implications, a field study was undertaken by us, though such a study is having serious limitations on account of the deeper involvement of various qualitative issues in the matter. The study was made in Kerala, the Malayalam speaking state in the Indian Union. Kerala is the most literate state in India. TV came to Kerala only in 1982 when a Low Power Transmitter was commissioned in Trivandrum on the eve of Asian Games. A High Power 10 KW Transmitter was set up in Trivandrum in 1985 with a studio complex coming up later in 1987. Since the liberalization of the economy and the opening of satellite channels in 1990s the progress was rapid. In close succession, many private channels were started one after another and as on today more than 17 channels transmit programmes in Malayalam. In addition, national channels like DD1, NDTV, multinational channels like BBC, CNN, STAR, and specialized channels like Planet World, Discovery, Pogo, Cartoon etc. are also in the field. The penetration of TV is equally widespread with as many as 3.73 million out of a total of 6.88 million households owning TV sets. Among the households owning TV sets, terrestrial TV homes number 2.28 and C&S TV homes number 1.45 million. Apparently, the penetration of satellite TV is not so widespread in comparison with some other states of the country.[10] It is estimated that members of nearly 61 percentage of the households watch TV. They watch regularly the programmes transmitted by the regional, national and international channels. According to another source TV reached 71.8 per cent of the population against only 67.1 percentage for news papers.[11]

The survey was held in Kerala during Jan-march 2007. Two hundred samples have been selected from all over the state for the survey by a combination of purposive and random sampling. The survey covered urban as well as rural areas. The samples are almost equally distributed between urban and rural areas. Males and females are also equally represented in the sample. Section 1 gives an account of the profile of the respondents and their viewing habits. In section 2 an account of the impact of television on the audience is given.

I
PROFILE OF THE RESPONDENTS AND THEIR VIEWING HABITS

Table 8.1: Demographic Profile of the Respondents

Age	*Urban*			*Rural*			*Total*		
	Male	*Female*	*Total*	*Male*	*Female*	*Total*	*Male*	*Female*	*Total*
10-19	3	6	9	2	1	3	5	7	12
20-29	16	17	33	20	36	56	37	52	89
30-39	8	7	15	9	10	19	17	17	34
40-49	9	8	17	3	8	11	12	16	28
50-59	12	8	20	3	2	5	15	10	25
60 & above	5	4	9	2	1	3	7	5	12
Total	53	50	103	39	58	97	93	107	200

The sample consists of 103 respondents from urban areas and 97 from rural areas. The sex wise distribution of the samples also was almost equal-97 are males and 103 are females. 88 per cent of the samples fall in the age group of 20-59, the rest 12 per cent of the respondents are equally distributed in the age groups of 10-19 and 60 and above. 45 per cent of the respondents are from the age group of 20-29.

The sample represents a cross section of the community—the respondents range from those with no formal education to those with the highest university degree. The respondents include people who are regularly employed, housewives, students, industrial and agricultural workers and retired persons. Table 8.2 below depicts the level of education of the respondents.

Table 8.2: Educational Qualification of the Respondents

	Urban	*Rural*	*Total*
No formal education	2	1	3
Below Std. 10	3	7	10
Std. 10-12	3	19	22
Undergraduates but HSc	18	15	33
Graduates and above	77	55	132
Total	103	97	200

More than 65 per cent of the respondents fall in the category of Graduates and above and 16 per cent in the category of undergraduates but H Sc. Respondents with no formal education is negligibly low, less than 2 per cent. The high literacy rate in the state could be the reason for the very low percentage of illiterates among the respondents. The educational profile of the audience is much higher in Kerala than that of the all India level. Though not comparable on account of methodological reasons, the NRS Survey of 1997 sheds some light on the educational profile of the audience in the country as a whole. According to it the educational qualification of the audience viewing DD1 has been as follows: illiterates 41.2 per cent, higher secondary and graduates combined 77 per cent and post grduates 79.4 per cent respectively.[12]

The social level of the respondents is reflected in their occupational distribution. In order to highlight this attribute the respondents have been classified on the basis of their occupation; see Table 8.3.

Table 8.3: Occupational Distribution of the Respondents

	Urban	*Rural*	*Total*
Service (Govt. and State)	33	10	33
Professional	12	0	12
Self Employed	2	2	2
Skilled worker	2	9	11
Farmer	0	1	1
Housewife	6	17	23
Student	32	50	82
Retired Person	12	2	14
Others	4	6	10
Total	103	97	200

Table 8.3 shows that the respondents represent a cross section of the community. The largest group among the respondents are students, constituting 41 per cent. They include those from the higher secondary level to post graduates (including research scholars). 21 per cent of the respondents are regularly employed either in government or private service. Housewives constitute more than 10 per cent of the respondents. Though not comparable on account of methodological reasons, the NRS Survey sheds some light on the break up of the audience on the basis of occupations. According to it, the occupational distribution of the audience of DD1 has been as follows: officer/executives 74.8; petty traders 53.8; shop owners 7.5; clerical/salaried 19.0; skilled 64.1 unskilled 48.9; students 8.5 and no work 63.2. The occupational distribution of audience of the other channels varied much from those of DD1.[13] The tastes and preferences of the respondents in respect of TV programmes vary from person to person. T V is just an entertainer to a large section of the population. Many others consider TV as an important source of national and international news. Sports, music and educational channels are of special interest to students and youngsters. The varying

interests of this group are adequately reflected in the sample by their greater representation.

The year of acquisition of TV is another factor which can also shed light on the involvement of TV in such matters.

Table 8.4: Year of Acquisition of TV by Respondents

Year	Urban	Rural	Total
Before 1995	75	40	115
1995-2000	23	31	54
After 2000	5	26	31
Total	103	97	200

In 95 per cent of the urban households and 71 per cent of the rural households in our sample TV made its entry before 2000. This shows that television became a popular visual medium in our households before the close of the last century.

Television remained a state monopoly in India till early 1990s. The state owned Doordarshan enjoyed exclusive monopoly for transmission of programmes. In 1990s private channels were given permission to operate in the country. Since then the number and coverage of private channels has shown a steady increase. Table 8.5 below gives details of cable connection among our respondents which enables them to view private channels.

Table 8.5: Cable Connection of the Respondents

	Respondents with Cable Connection	*Respondents without Cable Connection*	*Total*
Urban	88	15	103
Rural	68	29	97
Total	156	44	200

Table 8.5 shows that 88 per cent of the respondents in urban areas and nearly 70 per cent in rural areas have cable connection in their homes. This means that 78 per cent of the 200 respondents in the survey have cable connection. Private channels have become very popular among the households in

the state in less than a decade. This is evident from the fact that of the 156 respondents with cable connection, 40 per cent have acquired the connection before the year 2000; see Table 8.6.

Table 8.6: Year of Acquisition of Cable Connection by the Respondents

Year	*Urban*	*Rural*	*Total*
Before 2000	49	13	62
2001	11	13	24
2002	7	5	12
2003	6	12	18
2004	5	9	14
2005	6	10	16
2006	4	6	10
Total	88	68	156

As the Table shows 62 per cent of the respondents have acquired cable connection during the six year period of 2001 to 2006. Nevertheless a sizable section of the respondents had cable connection before the turn of the century.

Viewing Habits of the Respondents

As already indicated, TV has become the most sought after medium in most of the countries. All categories of people spend a portion of their time for watching TV programmes. Nevertheless the frequency of watching programmes vary from person to person. In order to ascertain the frequency of watching TV by the respondents we have classified them into three groups—those who watch TV regularly, frequently and occasionally; see Table 8.7.

Table 8.7: Frequency of Watching TV

Year	*Urban*	*Rural*	*Total*
Regularly (6-7 days a week)	62	65	127
Frequently (3-5 days a week)	24	13	37
Occasionally (1-2 days a week)	17	19	36
Total	103	97	200

The Table shows that 64 per cent of the respondents regularly watch TV, i.e.; 6 to 7 days a week.18 per cent of the respondents are in the habit of watching TV frequently, ie; 3 to 5 days a week. Another 18 per cent watch TV occasionally, i.e.; 1 to 2 days a week. It may be noted that those who watch TV regularly are equally divided between urban and rural areas. The proportion of people frequently watching TV varies to some extent according to the findings of an audience survey of Doordarshan Trivandum. Acording to their findings 78 per cent of the respondents watched TV regularly, 17.3 per cent frequently and 4.3 per cent occasionally.[14] The variation could be due to the differences in the universe adopted for sampling purpose A sex wise classification of data shows that among those who regularly watch TV women outnumber men; see Table 8.8.

Table 8.8: Frequency of Watching TV—Sex wise Classification

Year	*Male*	*Female*	*Total*
Regularly (6-7 days a week)	54	73	127
Frequently (3-5 days a week)	21	16	37
Occasionally (1-2 days a week)	18	18	36
Total	93	107	200

Of the 107 women respondents 68 per cent regularly watch TV. They constitute 57 per cent of the 127 respondents in the group. This is in accordance with the general impression that women spent more time before the visual media than men.

Among the regular viewers of TV 33 per cent spent 1-2 hours a day before TV and 26 per cent spent 2-3 hours. The details are given in Table 8.9.

It is seen that 20 per cent of the viewers earmark less than one hour for TV programmes.18 per cent of the respondents spent 3 to 5 hours a day before TV. In the case of the nominal 3.5 per cent of the respondents who watch programmes for more than 5 hours a day TV is perhaps an addiction. Except in the category of those who watch programmes for 1 to 2 hours a day, there is no significant difference between urban and rural respondents regarding the time earmarked for viewing TV. If

Table 8.9: Time Spent in a Day for Watching TV

	Urban	*Rural*	*Total*
Less than 1 hour	22	18	40 (20)
1-2 hours	41	24	65 (32.5)
2-3 hours	25	27	27 (13.5)
3-4 hours	8	18	25 (12.5)
4-5 hours	4	7	11 (5.5)
More than 5 hours	4	3	7 (3.5)
Total	103	97	200 (100)

we assume that the viewing time is uniformly distributed the total viewing time would be only 360.5 hours. That means the respondents spend on an average 1 hour and 48 minutes per day or 12.6 hours per week On the other hand, it is reported that a person used to spend on an average 133 minutes per day for watching TV in the country as a whole.[15] On the other hand,, the Americans used to view on an average 31 hours a week and the Britishers 26 hours a week during 1980s. Only the Dutch among the Westerners used to watch 12 hours a week in 1985.[16] The time spent for viewing television is much lower than that of the developed nations of the West, apparently on account of the non availability of leisure time.

The data pertaining to time spent before TV by the respondents in our survey show that women spent more time for viewing before TV than men; see Table 8.10.

Table 8.10: Time Spent in a Day for Watching TV—Sex wise Distribution of the Respondents

	Male	*Female*	*Total*
Less than one hour	23	17	40
1-2 hours	34	31	65
2-3 hours	20	32	52
3-4 hours	10	15	25
4-5 hours	4	7	11
More than 5 hours	2	5	7
Total	93	107	200

It is seen that among those who spent more than 2 hours a day, women outnumber men. There is no significant difference in their proportion in the category of those who watch TV from 1 to 2 hours. The female respondents on an average spend 2 hours and 18 minutes per day for viewing television prorammes. On the other hand, male respondents spend on an average 1 hour and 22 minutes for viewing programmes.

It is believed that people spend more time during peak hours for viewing TV programmes. Accordingly data on the time spent during the prime time was also collected. The information obtained is presented in Table 8.11.

Table 8.11: Daily Watching Time of Watching Television

	Urban	*Rural*	*Total*
6 a.m. to 8 a.m.	2	6	8
8 a.m. to 10 a.m.	3	2	5
10 a.m. to 12 a.m.	2	1	3
12 a.m. to 3 p.m.	6	4	10
3 p.m. to 6 p.m.	7	14	21
6 p.m. to 8 p.m.	33	26	59
8 p.m. to 10 p.m.	44	40	84
10 p.m. to 6 a.m.	6	4	10
Total	103	97	200

42 per cent of the respondents have reported that they usually watch television between 8 p.m. and 10 p.m. and nearly 30 per cent between 6 p.m. and 8 p.m. Thus 6 p.m. to 10 p.m. is the prime time of the respondents for watching television. After a day's routine work this is the time available to view programmes in television. Entertainment and informative programmes scheduled during this time period also make it the prime time. No significant difference exists between urban and rural respondents in the case of prime time. During prime time it is found that more women than men watch television; see Table 8.12.

55 per cent of the 143 viewers of television during prime time are women. Between 3 p.m and 6 p.m. also women exceed men among the viewers. Popular films, film songs, soap operas and serials are the among the programmes telecast during

Table 8.12: Daily Watching Time of Television—Sex wise Distribution

	Male	*Female*	*Total*
6 a.m. to 8 a.m.	5 (5)	3 (3)	8 (4)
8 a.m. to 10 a.m.	4 (4)	1 (1)	5 (3)
10 a.m. to 12 a.m.	2 (2)	1 (1)	3 (2)
12 a.m. to 3 p.m.	5 (5)	5 (5)	10 (5)
3 p.m. to 6 p.m.	7 (8)	14 (13)	21 (10)
6 p.m. to 8 p.m.	23 (25)	36 (33)	59 (29)
8 p.m. to 10 p.m.	41 (44)	43 (40)	84 (42)
10 p.m. to 6 a.m.	6 (7)	4 (4)	10 (5)
Total	93 (100)	107 (100)	200 (100)

prime time. Women appear to have a special preference for these programmes. This accounts for their greater proportion among the prime time viewers.

Though Doordarshan is the first television channel in the country, private channels enjoy greater patronage from the viewers. Among our respondents only a small proportion access programmes in Doordarshan; see Table 8.13. Among the 200 respondents in our survey, it has been found that those who watch Doordarshan channels is less than 40 per cent.

Table 8.13: Doordarshan Channels Usually Watched by Respondents

	Urban	*Rural*	*Total*
DD1	16	19	35
DD Regional	10	14	24
DD Sports	5	1	6
DD News	6	5	11
Other DD Channels	2	1	3
Total	39	40	79

It may be noted from the Table that the viewers of Doordarshan channels are almost equally distributed between urban and rural areas. The most commonly watched channels are DD1 and DD Regional. The number of respondents who watch other Doordarshan channels are relatively very small in urban as well as rural areas. It could be ascertained that the DTH service launched by Doordarshan has not made any visible impact so far. Only a small percentage among our respondents have DTH connection.

Preference to Programmes

Over the years the visual media have become highly competitive. As a result there has been a deliberate attempt on the part of the channels to add new varieties of programmes. Programmes catering to the tastes and preferences of the viewers are being introduced on an increasing scale. We have made an attempt during the survey to ascertain the preferences of the viewers with respect to the programmes appearing in the TV. For this purpose, the programmes have been classified into three categories viz informative, educative and entertaining. News, reports, current affairs, talks and discussions were included under informative programmes; quiz, health and family welfare programmes, adult education, school TV programmes meant for women, youth and workers under educative programmes; and serials, music, dance, features, films, skits, cartoons, and sports under entertainment programmes.

The respondents in certain cases have expressed their difficulty to differentiate the programmes exclusively as informative, educative, or entertaining. In view of the nature of the programmes presented in TV this difficulty appears to be genuine. However it is obvious that programmes like news or current affairs are informative and programmes relating to health nd family welfare are educative. Similarly serials, films and music are more valued for their entertainment element. The preference of the viewers in respect of different programmes can be known from the type of programmes which they usually watch. The Table 8.14 gives the information pertaining to this aspect.

It may be noted that entertainment programmes have the largest number of viewers followed by informative programmes. More than three-fourth of the respondents regularly watch entertainment programmes along with other programmess. Informative programmes are watched by almost

Table 8.14: Audiences' Preference to Programmes

	Informative	*Educational*	*Entertainment*
Male	82	27	69
Female	66	44	93
Total	148	71	162

an equal percentage of viewers. There are 71 respondents who regularly watch educational programmes. The gender wise classification shows that entertainment programmes are more popular among women and informative programmes among men 93 out of 107 female respondents regularly watch entertainment programmes and 82 out of 93 men regularly watch informative progrmmes.

II
IMPACT OF TELEVISION

Being a visual media television is capable of creating a direct and immediate impact in the minds of viewers. The impact of the visual media is multi-dimensional extending over social and economic spheres. We have identified four different areas namely, social relationship and involvement in social activities, reading habits, consumption habits and food habits in which the impact of television is visibly felt, for empirical analysis in our study. In addition television also serves as a source of news and as an entertainer.

Social Relationship and Involvement in Social Activities

The impact of television on social relationship and involvement in social activities and reading habits is a widely debated issue. People who are interested in regularly watching serials and entertainment programmes telecast over visual media as per a notified schedule often get tied up to television. Neither do they make social visits, nor do they welcome social visits to their household. They even avoid social and family functions. In their case, it becomes difficult to maintain regular social relationship.

Involvement in social activities is a time consuming affair. Only those who have a social concern and vision will be able to set apart a part of their time for social activities. People who get addicted to TV programmes will be less interested to get involved in social activities. But there are people who claim that programmes in TV have improved their social relationship and involvement in social activities. During the survey we have ascertained from the viewers whether regular watching of TV has had any impact on their social relationship and involvement in social activities. We have looked at the impact from three dimensions; ie, whether there has been any improvement, decline or no change in the social relationship. Table 8.15 gives a summary of the responses obtained from the viewers.

Table 8.15: Changes in Social Relationship and Social Involvement among Television Viewers

(Figures in percentages)

	Improved	*Declined*	*No change*	*Total*
Urban	33	18	49	100
Rural	43	17	40	100
Total	38	18	44	100

44 per cent of the respondents claim that regular watching of TV has in no way affected their social relationship, 49 per cent among them are from urban areas and 40 per cent are from rural areas. Among the 38 per cent who claim that their social relationship has improved 33 per cent are from urban areas and 43 per cent are from rural areas. 18 per cent of the respondents who admit a decline in their social relationship are almost equally divided between urban and rural areas. We may now look into the impact on social relationship among men and women. For this purpose a sex wise break up of the data is presented in Table 8.16.

42 per cent of the male respondents and 35 per cent of female respondents claim that their social relationship has improved while 19 per cent of men and 17 per cent of women state there is a decline in their social relationship, 40 per cent of men and 48 per cent of women have stated that there is no change in their social relationship.

Table 8.16: Changes in Social Relationship and Social Involvement among Television Viewers Sex wise Classification (Figures in percentages)

	Improved	*Declined*	*No change*	*Total*
Males	42	19	40	100
Females	35	17	48	100
Total	36	18	44	100

Reading Habit

Reading habit is another casualty of the growing popularity of television. Television is a source of news as well as a source of knowledge. Before the advent of television, books, journals and news papers were the sources of news and knowledge. To those who rely on media for news and knowledge, reading is no attraction. We have tried to ascertain whether there has been any change in the reading habit of the respondents as a result of regular watching of TV. Table 8.17 presents the information collected.

Table 8.17: Changes in Reading Habit

(Figures in percentages)

	Improved	*Declined*	*No change*	*Total*
Urban	29	42	29	100
Rural	24	41	35	100
Total	28	41	32	100

41 per cent of the respondents have stated that their reading habit has declined after they started to watch television regularly; their proportion is almost the same in urban and rural areas. 32 per centof the respondents, 29 per cent and 35 per cent respectively from urban areas and rural areas, testify that there has been no change in their reading habit. Among the 28 per cent who claim that their reading habit has improved, 29 per cent are urban respondents and 24 per cent are rural respondents. The data presented above show that there has been a decline in the reading habit of a sizable group. A sex wise

classification of the data gives almost the same picture; see Table 8.18.

Table 8.18: Changes in Reading Habits Sex wise Classification

(Figures in percentages)

	Improved	*Declined*	*No change*	*Total*
Urban	30	43	28	100
Rural	23	40	37	100
Total	27	41	32	100

Among the 41 per cent who have testified that their reading habit has declined, 43 per cent are males and 40 per cent are females.30 per cent males and 23 per cent females have stated that their reading habit has improved.28 per cent from among men and 37 per cent from among women are of the opinion that there is no change in their reading habit. The growing popularity of television has resulted in a decline in the reading habit of a section of both men and women.

Advertisement and Consumption Habits

Advertisement has a two fold role in a market economy—informative and promotional. It is through advertisement that the producer conveys the information pertaining to a new product. Once the product is launched the producer uses advertisement as a means to promote sales by highlighting the special qualities of the product. Advertisement in the visual media takes the message to a wider spectrum. Hence it has become an effective means of promoting sales. Advertisement influences the consumption habits of the viewers through its impact on the kind and volume of goods purchased.

We have made an attempt to ascertain whether consumption habits in the household have been influenced by advertisement in television. The views expressed by the respondents are presented in Table 8.19.

Table 8.19: Advertisement and Consumption Habits

(Figures in percetages)

	Yes	*No*	*Total*
Urban	45	55	100
Rural	45	55	100
Total	45	55	100

45 per cent of the respondents have stated that their consumption habits have been influenced by advertisement in the visual media. There is no significant difference between urban and rural areas in the proportion of respondents who agree to have been influenced by advertisement in their consumption habits.

The impact of advertisement on consumption habits appears to be greater among women. A sex wise break up of the data supports this contention; see Table 8.20.

Table 8.20: Advertisement and Consumption Habits (Sex wise Classification)

(Figures in percentages)

	Yes	*No*	*Total*
Male	42	58	100
Female	48	52	100
Total	45	55	100

48 per cent of women have reported that their consumption habits have been influenced by advertisement while the proportion of men who testifies to the influence is 42 per cent. The proportion of men and women who are not influenced by advertisement are 58 per cent and 52 per cent respectively.

Impact on Food Habits

Television may influence the food habits in a household in two ways. Influenced by advertisements the kind and volume of goods purchased in a household may undergo a change. It is also likely that TV programmes may reduce the time available for cooking and people may go for hotel food or ready-made cooked items. Table 8.21 below gives the details of change that has taken place among our respondents in respect of food habits.

Table 8.21: Television's Influence on Food Habits

(Figures in percentage)

	Yes	*No*	*Total*
Urban	24	76	100
Rural	14	86	100
Total	20	80	100

Only 20 percent of the respondents have admitted that television has brought about a change in their food habits. Twentyfour per cent among them are from urban households and 14 per cent from rural households. It could be ascertained that a sexwise classification did not show any significant variation from the general pattern

Television as a Source of News

There are few people who do not have a sense of the rest of the world. They may not be highly knowledgeable, they may have little more than flickering images in front of their mind's eye. But chances are that their sense of what is going on elsewhere on the planet is derived from television, so also their sense of the key moments in history.[17] This points to the role of television as a source of news.

Over the last four decades television has become very popular among the masses in India. With the increase in the number of channels common people began to rely more on the visual media for the news on the latest events in the national and international scene. The 24 hour news service by different channels brings the latest news to every household which has access to television. It is no wonder that the majority of respondents in our survey have given a high rating for the role of television as a source of news; see Table 8.22.

Table 8.22: Role of Television as a Source of News

(Figures in Percentages)

	High	*Low*	*Nil*	*Total*
Urban	90	8	2	100
Rural	91	8	1	100
Total	91	8	1	100

More than 90 per cent of the respondents have rated high the role of television as a source of news. Those who have given low rating is only 8 per cent and 'Nil' rating a negligible 1 per cent. There is practically no difference between urban and rural respondents in their rating. We may now examine the rating by men and women with respect to the role of television as a source of news; see Table 8.23.

Table 8.23: Role of Television as a Source of News (Sex wise Classification)

(Figures in Percentages)

	High	*Low*	*Nil*	*Total*
Male	94	5	1	100
Female	88	10	2	100
Total	91	8	1	100

The rating by both men and women on the role of television as a source of news is high, but men give a higher rating of 94 per cent and women a slightly lower rating of 88 per cent. Obviously the role of television as a source of news is universally recognized irrespective of gender and the place of residence. Wherever people have access to television they value its role in conveying the news on national and international events.

Television as an Entertainer

Entertainment on television is not a distinct genre but a continuum of regular programmes which include serials, soap operas, game shows, quizzes and variety shows. Entertainment offers available pleasures in the face of the problems of life. This can be seen as reconciling audiences to the status quo; or, as a way to lead people to question and criticize the status quo by reference to the ideal world in the entertainment utopia.[18] Whatever be the ultimate outcome, to the common man entertainment comes as a relief from the dreariness of everyday life. During the course of the primary survey we have made an attempt to elicit the views our respondents on the role of television as an entertainer. Table 8.24 presents the rating of the role of television as an entertainer by the respondents.

Table 8.24: Role of Television as an Entertainer

(Figures in Percentages)

	High	*Low*	*Nil*	*Total*
Urban	87	10	3	100
Rural	91	9	0	100
Total	89	10	1	100

Nearly 90 per cent of the respondents have rated high the role of television as entertainer; 87 per cent among them are from urban areas and 91 per cent from rural areas. Those who give low rating are 10 per cent, almost equally divided between urban and rural areas. Those who give 'Nil' rating is a negligible 1 per cent.

How important is television as entertainer to the viewers is brought out by the data presented in the table. A sex wise classification shows that it is women more than men who value the role of television as entertainer; see Table 8.25

Table 8.25: Role of Television as an Entertainer (Sex wise Classification)

(Figures in Percentages)

	High	*Low*	*Nil*	*Total*
Male	85	12	3	100
Female	93	7	0	100
Total	89	10	1	100

93 per cent of women respondents in the survey have given high rating to the role of television as entertainer. The corresponding proportion among men is 85 per cent, 12 per cent among men and 7 per cent among women give low rating. The data testifies to the general impression that the entertainment programmes in television attracts more women than men.

Conclusion

Within the last thirty years of its arrival, TV has grown as an integral part of the social life of the people of Kerala. TV provides a wide variety of menu comprising cookery shows of delicious food, hot news, heated political discussions, mega-serials, spot relay of cricket matches, film shows, local gossips and so on for the consumption of the audience. Apparently the audiences who have cultivated television viewing as a habit eagerly watch the programmes. Women rather than men are in front of the TV set for more hours. However the craze for sitting in front of the TV has not become as virulent as in the West if the shorter duration of time spent in front of the TV is taken as the criterion

The impact of TV viewing has been very powerful by all standards. The consumerist culture which TV propagates has become part and parcel of the life style in Kerala. TV can cause immense harm to society by promoting unethical themes and projecting crime, violence and sex. Children who are keen watchers of TV can become the targets of such evil influence of TV. What the society should do to safeguard itself against such evil effects of TV forms the theme of the next chapter.

NOTES AND REFERENCES

1. Conrad, Lodziak (1986). *The Power of Television; A Critical Appraisal,* London, Frances Pinter (Publishers), p. 140.
2. Jonathan, Bignell (2004) in *An Introduction to Television Studies,* p. 264 quotes from Hartley, J. *Tele-ology; Studies in Television,* London Routledge.

3. Jonathan, Bignell (2004). *op. cit.*, p. 26.
4. Gandy, Oscar H. (2004). "Audience on Demand" in Calabrese Andrew and Sparks Colm (ed.) *Towards a Political Economy of Culture*, Oxford, UK, Brown and Field Publishers, p. 327.
5. Barker, Chiris (1997). *Global Television an Introduction*, Oxford Blackwell Publishers, p. 115.
6. Bob, Mullan (1997). *Consuming Television*, Oxford, Blackwell Publishers, p. 18.
7. Jonathan, Bignell (2004). *op. cit.*, p. 264.
8. Conrad, Lodziak (1986). *op. cit.*, p. 135.
9. Shanahan and Morgan (1999). *Television and its Viewers; Cultivation Theory and Research*, Cambridge, University Press.
10. GOI Doordarshan Kendra Thiruvananthapuram A Profile June 2007.
11. Venkeiteswaran, C.S. (2007). "The Science of Media Facts" in *Indian Express*, 18 August 2007 based on Kerala Sastra Sahitya Parishad's survey in 2006.
12. David, Page and William, Crawley (2001). *Satellite Over South Asia: Broadcasing Culture and Public Interest*, New Delhi, Sage Publications, p. 123.
13. David, Page and William, Crawley (2001). *op. cit.*, p. 124.
14. Doordarshan Kendra Trivandrum (2005). *TV Viewrship Survey Thiruvananthapuram (Audience Research Unit).*
15. *Doordarshan India 2002.*
16. Susan, Briggs (1995). "Television in the Home and Family" in Smith Anthony (ed.); *Television an Intenational History*, Oxford University Press, p. 111.
17. Tracey, Michael (1998). "Non-fiction Television" in Smith, Antony (ed.) *Television an International History*, New York, Oxford University Press, p. 6.
18. Patterson, Richard (1998). "Drama and Entertainment" in Smith Antony (ed.), *op. cit.*, p. 64.

9

Policy Options in Television Industry

We have seen in the previous chapters, how television which falls within the ambit of culture industry is concerned with the creation and transmission of texts which are creative products carrying symbolic meanings. Notwithstanding the cultural moorings of its products, television which is organized on factory lines provides employment to a large number of people and creates substantial volume of income wherever it has grown. The texts themselves which are transmitted as programmes, are produced in such a way as to get maximum returns through advertisement by attracting as many number of viewers as possible. In so doing, television becomes more of an economic activity in which economic parameters like capital, investment, marketing, profit, play key roles in its functioning. With the ongoing process of liberalization and globalization, which advocates laissez-faire capitalism with very little state interference in the realm of economic world, state has withdrawn from the commanding position as the informer, educator and entertainer through television. At the same time, with the development of satellite technology programme from any part of the world can penetrate easily in other parts. National frontiers have thus become irrelevant in controlling the entry of TV programmes from outside the country. In the wake of such developments, most of the governments have adopted a laissez-faire policy in so far as television is concerned. Proliferation of channels has become a reality and with each channel carrying signals far and wide, it has become difficult to control even programmes originating within the country. Under such circumstances, the question is, should the state leave everything to the free play of the market? Is not the state the custodian of the interests of the society at large? Does not the state have a moral obligation to safeguard the well-being of the citizens by regulating and even interfering in an enterprise like television which has grown as an important cultural instrument whose products still carry cultural flavour though diluted by the overflow of economic norms? If so, what should be the yardsticks and how they are to be applied are the questions posed? The theme of this chapter is to seek answer to the aforesaid questions posed.

TV the One Eyed Monster

What the channels do, is to broadcast a wide variety of entertainment programmes. They are produced in such a way as to attract maximum number of audience or for meeting the requirements of a mass audience. Cultural side is being marginalised for the purpose of securing more income. In reality, they are pure commercial products. Very often, the language, the presentation and the theme are suitably formulated in such a way as to meet the commercial requirements. Invariably, vulgar themes with obscene language get undue importance in any programme. Sex and violence are also projected with impunity in many cases. Producers of the programme justify the presentation of sex and violence, as a natural outcome of freedom of expression. Their contention seems to be untenable, as most of such works are devoid of cultural contents. They are to put in the words of Fischer, "the corrupting evil filth of capitalist pulp art".[1] Needless to say, programmes of such a nature are potent with undesirable and even dangerous consequences. They can undermine social values and stimulate people to indulge in violence or to harass women for sexual indulgences. TV has been accused as the instigator of the increased incidence of violence, sexual assault, divorce, etc. discerning during recent years. In such cases, the state as the guardian of the public interest has an obligation to step in.

Undesirable consequences can also stem from the

presentation of news. Instances are numerous where live telecast of sensational news can stir people for violent reaction. Some items of the live telecast of the terrorist attack in Mumbai on 26th November 2008 were not helpful to the cause national interest. As reported in the Hindu, even the Chief justice of India was not satisfied with the way in which the events were telecast by some of the channels. In his words "the symbolic impact of terrorists attack on the minds of ordinary citizens has also been considerably amplified by the role of pervasive media coverage".[2]

A far more serious aspect of the issue relates to the impact of television on children. Television has grown to such an extent as to become an integral part of modern life in most parts of the world. As already mentioned, people spend more time in watching programmes in the TV than for any other purpose. With the widespread penetration of TV, children are invariably found in front of the TV for most of the time. According to a UK study of 1996 in collaboration with twelve other European nations, TV has become the most popular leisure time for children who spend on an average 147 minutes a day for watching TV as against 45 minutes for video, 28 minutes for books and 31 minutes for non-game computer.[3] Similarly, according to another study, an American child on an average would have spent 20,000 hours watching television against only 11,000 hours in the classroom by the time he completes his school education.[4] Furthermore, TV has become some sort of a baby sitter in many cases. The following statement of a girl of 12 sheds light on how TV operates as a baby sitter: "When my little brother comes home from school, and he is totally worn out and mum needs to cook the tea, she will pull him up in front of the telly for half an hour because he is too worn out to do anything active and then when he 's watched a couple of programmes, she says why don't you do some drawing or something."[5] When TV is thus such an inseparable companion., it would certainly be playing a key role in moulding the behavioural pattern and character formation of youngsters. At the same time, programmes specially prepared for children do not have much of an audience response. Channels compensate this as in the case of other programmes with an overdose of suitable advertisements, very often with an embedded persuasion capable of attracting the attention of children. Needless to say, the advertisements are as much powerful, if not more as the programmes in influencing the children.

Apparently, children have to be protected from falling victims to the evil influence of television. The need for protection becomes stronger for various reasons. First, children are an immature class who do not have sufficient knowledge to make a proper judgement on any matter. Second, they can be easily influenced, as they possess very little experience in the world. In fact, television can easily confuse people particularly children into making them believe what they see on TV as the real truth. Internalization of new ideas is very quick with children. Needless to say, the habits formed during childhood cannot easily be changed at a later period. Very often, the media operators look upon them as another market segment and try to sell their products by influencing the children through advertisements. For them, it is an investment for the future which the manufacturers expect will pay off many times over.[6] Fourth, many of the programmes create a bad impression in the minds of children. Children easily become addicts to violence and such other evil activities by seeing such TV programmes. A typical instance is the murder of a two-year boy, James Bulger in Liverpool in 1993. The boy was abducted by two ten year olds, John Venable and Robert Thompson who tortured and brutally murdered him. It was alleged that the boy was killed by the senior boys who seem to have been inspired to do the cruel act from what they saw in some TV scenes, though it was not conclusively proved that the murder took place by emulating the examples portrayed in television. Nevertheless, there was a hue and cry in the press with the accusing finger on TV programmes. Even John Major, the then British Prime Minister did not hesitate to comment "on the relentless diet of violence" and "its serious effects on the young."[7] A similar apprehension on the adverse impact of TV was expressed in a stronger language by the US Senator Robert Byrd, when he stated in 1991 as follows: "if we in this nation continue to sow the images of murder, violence, drug abuse, sadism, arrogance, irreverence, blasphemy, perversion, pornography, and aberration before the eyes of millions of children, year after year, day after day, we should not be surprised if the foundation of the society rot away as if from leprosy".[8] In other words, immense harm is being done in the society by broadcasting such harmful scenes which inculcate a criminal mentality in the minds of children. In sum, TV is termed in the words of an author, as the "one eyed monster" which snatches away the children in its maw and nurtures them as some kind of monsters.[9]

Nevertheless, some authors maintain that television does not in any way contribute to the growth of violence in the society. Viewing the violent scenes on the other hand, can in fact create a cathartic effect. It can in turn, lead to a better understanding and appreciation of real conditions of life. Some writers even claimed that they could even produce creative works from the experience they gained by seeing such horror scenes during their younger days. In the opinion of Messenger, who has made a study on the impact of TV on children, some of the forbidden taboos would disappear, if the children are allowed to see the representation of sex and violence more freely in the early childhood.[10]

On the other hand, practically almost all the studies conclude that TV is instrumental in creating undesirable consequences in the behavioural pattern of people particularly young children. Most of them bring to lime-light, the evil consequences arising from viewing sex and violence which are portrayed lavishly in TV. According to the findings of a study by the US National Coalition in 1992 on Television Violence "over sixty percent of the music videos contained at least one of the following elements; explicit violence, suggestions of violence, degrading sexual portrayals, sexually suggestive themes, profanity, etc.". in networks like MTV which broadcast such themes over 29 instances on an average per hour. Unnikrishnan and Bajpai who quote this passage enjoin that the target audience of MTV type networks is children, teenagers and young adults.[11] Needless to say, the exposure of children to such dangerous themes could be dangerous in the long run. In the wake of Bulger murder, Elizabeth Newson, a child psychologist who made a study in the matter expressed that the professionals in child health and psychology under estimated the degree of brutality and sustained sadism portrayed in the films and the interest with which children watch such programmes. In her opinion, what is experienced vicariously, will have effect on some people. Furthermore, she felt that some parents cannot be trusted to restrict the children's viewing habits and society must take on the responsiblity in protecting children from such matters through active censorship.[12] Miles Rosalind, another scholar who made a study in the matter, maintains that the pernicious influence of video nasties will not be fully manifested for a generation or more to come. She adds further and states that the images sink into the great quagmire of unconscious where they work a way unseen.[13] In an international collection of essays on children and media violence, edited by two women and published by UNESCO in 1998, the authors accept as axiomatic that adult society should be concerned about children and their relationship with images of people being "shot, knifed, blown up or raped before their eyes". The authors who approached the issue from different disciplinary angles, were unanimous in their opinion that children are vulnerable to it and that national and international regulations are required to protect children from it.[14]

Another problematic aspect of visual representation of violence whether playful or not is the strength of persistence of images in memory. Messenger who examined the whole issue of censorship enjoins further, "memory may remove the narrative context of a filmed event but will retain images of skin flailing tortures for many months, even years during which the image may be recalled divorced from the moral context of the story. Such decontextualised memories can be very disturbing."[15]

According to another author television is seen sometimes

as a mainlining injection of anti-social values into the home against which children need to be defended and immunized.[16] Messenger who was not enthusiastic about outright censorship came to the conclusion that the need to make special provision for children through the design and regulation of the technology was even more necessary than it might have been in the past.[17]

Since the impact of violent scenes and such other things are not so simple, children should be protected from seeing such kinds of programmes. At the same time, they have to be provided with correct information. Article 17 of the UN Convention on the Right of the Child, stresses on "the role of media in disseminating information to children that is consistent with moral well-being and knowledge and understanding among people and respects the child's cultural background and the state is to take measures to encourage this and to protect children from harmful materials".[18] Though the convention stipulates the protection of children as a duty of the parents, state also is called upon to protect the children from the harmful materials. Apparently, it is a pertinent question whether the state or parents are to be the protectors of children from harmful materials flowing from the media. Since TV is potentially capable of adversely affecting the children, they have to be protected from anything and everything shown on TV.

Apart from the adverse emotional impact, television viewing is bad to the brain and health of the children. TV can very well impair children's power of concentration. It is reported that every extra hour of television watching a day may lead to attentional difficulties upto 9 per cent in the case of children. As Oliver James reports further "a 26-year study of 1,000 children showed that those who watched more than two-hours a day between five and fifteen were significantly, unhealthier years later."[19] Needless to say, the need for protecting the children from too much exposure from TV becomes all the more serious. Apparently, how to protect the children from such adverse effects of TV is a serious problem.

Audience View on Control and Regulation

In view of the seriousness of the issue, the audiences themselves were asked to indicate their opinion regarding the desirability of introducing control on the programmes. Needless to say, programmes are targeted at the audience. The survey as stated in the previous chapter, was made during January-March 2007 in Trivandrum, Quilon and Alleppey districts of Kerala. Among the respondents, 58 per cent of them indicated the need for control on production and transmission of programmes. Interestingly, 58 per cent among the males and females alike were in favour of control. Those who were against any control formed 42 per cent. The opposition to controls came mainly from the youngsters in the age group 20-29 who alone formed more than 44 percent of the total respondents.

Majority of the channels are in the private sector. All of them engage in a tough competition for retaining their hold in the market. Since their interest is to earn maximum profit by attracting a large size of audience, they invariably indulge in the production progrmmes with vulgar themes which are harmful to the society at large. The respondents were asked to indicate whether more stringent controls should be imposed on private channels. The answer was positive. However, only 57 per cent of the respondents were in favour of stringent laws to regulate private channels. However 62 per cent of the females favoured stringent measures against only 53 per cent of the males favouring stringent regulations.

Another question relates to the attitude of audience towards imposing stricter controls on advertisements. The harmful effects of advertisements are far more serious than that of regular programmes. On this question, 76 per cent of the respondents favoured greater control against only 24 per cent giving a negative response. However, 80 per cent of the males against only 72 per cent of the females were in favour stricter controls. Thus majority of the respondents were in favour of stricter controls on programnmes and also on advertisements.

How to Bell the Cat

One of the methods is to regulate the timing of the programmes under what is known as "family viewing policy" adopted in some countries. In Great Britain the practice is to show adult programme after 9'o clock in the evening. Such a system is adopted on the assumption that children will go to bed by 9 P.M. However, there are many difficulties inherent with the system as most of the children are very curious people. They will try to see the programme after parents have gone to bed. A girl of 10 for instance, made the following remarks on this aspect; "If my dad says that I am not allowed to watch it, I will just wait till he's gone to bed and I will watch it on the video in my room".[20] An Indian author apprehended the possibility of such a situation and stated in clear terms that "there is a moral panic among parents with satellite channels, especially Channel V and MTV, in the lower middle class, where parents say they are afraid to leave the home and go away because children will turn to these channels".[21] When there is a prohibition the curiosity will be stronger. Interestingly, a 10 year girl is stated to have observed that "I like watching blood thirsty and action packed films on Sky. I would like more action packed stories to be on the television."[22] They will be able to see the programme through the video also. Since most of children in the developed countries are provided with separate TV sets of their own, the implementation of the regulatory system becomes difficult.

Another method is to impose a code on the exhibition of programmes. The broadcasters in our country are bound to follow the provisions of the Advertising and Programming code. However, many of the channels may not be adhering to the code. In such cases, government will have to step in and ban the transmission. The ban imposed on the transmission and retransmission of La Cosy Underwear and Amul Macho Underwear on the ground that that they were indecent, vulgar and suggestive is a typical instance of the direct entry of the government in this matter.[23] However, the violation of the code comes to the notice only after the actual transmission. All the programme cannot be watched before imposing the code. The proposed Content Code making the regulations more explicit would be a step in the right direction. Though the channels have been critical of the code, it is sure to have positive effect on TV programmes.

One of the options which the state can adopt is to impose censorship. It was a weapon adopted from ancient past. Modern governments also impose censorship though not as frequently as in the past. The fatwa issued by Iranian authorities against Sulman Rushdie, for his work *Satanic Verses* is a classical instance of censorship. Censorship per se, has been criticized for various reasons. Indiscriminate use of censorship can curtail artistic freedom of expression. On many occasions, ruling classes have tried to suppress artistic works which were critical to their behaviour and action. Suppression of dissent with censorship can also hamper social progress.

Censorship is being adopted in our country in the case of films. No film can be exhibited without getting the clearance from the Censor Board. They in turn, classify the films as fit to be shown to all classes of people or to adults only and so on. The system of censorship is criticized as an attempt to curtail artistic freedom by the exponents of commercial cinema. As already mentioned, most of the films are commercial commodities with very little cultural content. Apparently, when censorship is imposed on such films as "it is not art that is being restricted by any censorship, but commercial practices".[24] State as the guardian of the society has a moral obligation to safeguard the interests of the citizens. Even otherwise, state has an obligation to safeguard the interests of the public as consumers. Most of the filth which comes through the TV are meant for public consumption. They can harm the society in injecting contents which poison the mind. As in the case of noise control or pollution control, state has a moral responsibility to protect the citizens from such poisonous elements.

The problem is, how to introduce censorship when as many as 260 and odd channels transmit programmes continuously in our country. The problem becomes a bit complicated because many of the programmes are relayed by foreign channels. State authorities come to know of the programme after it is relayed. The retention of censorship in the statue is highly desirable as it can be used as and when the occasion arises.

Another measure which can be adopted, is to ban certain programmes. According Article 19 of the Cable Act, the public authorities can prohibit the transmission of any programme, if it is likely to promote on grounds of religion, race, language, caste or community or any other ground whatsoever, disharmony or feelings of enmity, hatred, or ill-will, between different religions, racial, or linguistic or regional groups, or castes or communities or which is likely to disturb the public tranquility.[25] However, the article speaks in general terms only and does not contemplate how to safeguard from the evil influence of TV.

Unlimited Entry of Channels

Though not directly connected with the quality of the contents or the mechanism of regulations, an equally important issue relates to the number of channels. With the withdrawal of regulations, the number of channels has been increasing every day. As on today, there are as many as 261 channels beaming programmes in India. Then the problem is, can there be sufficient scope for such a large number of channels. Their known sources of income are receipts from advertisements and a share of the receipts from the cable channels. There is a limit upto which advertisement can sustain the industry. However, the problem becomes complicated because they deal with works of art which cannot be left entirely to the market forces alone. The problem is how to regulate or to put the programmes on the correct track.

The options which the state can exercise are circumscribed by the pulls from different directions. Nevertheless, state has a moral obligation to safeguard the interests of the society at large than to keep mum on the profiteering approach of the channels. Significantly, even the Committee on Petitions of the Rajya Sabha arrived at a conclusion in favour of statutory regulations on the media in the larger interest of the society as indicated in its 132 Report tabled on 12 December 2008. In their opinion, self regulation forms an ideal measure. However. it might not be effective in regulating the media particularly in the scenario of growing competition amongst the channels for supremacy in the business of ratings.[26] As mentioned earlier, the findings of the field survey conducted by us also corroborate the need for control over TV programmes. However, the options have to be pursued cautiously by drawing well thought out strategy. Enlightened public opinion can be the main source from which the state can draw much of its inspiration in the matter.

NOTES AND RREFERENCES

1. Ernst, Fischer (1959). *Necessity of Art: A Marxist Approach,* Penguin Books, p. 207.
2. *The Hindu,* 14th December, 2008.
3. Messenger Maire Davies (2001). *Dear BBC. Children, Television. Story Telling and Public Sphere,* Cambridge, University Press, p. 21.
4. Bob, Mullan (1997). *Consuming Television,* Oxford Blackwell Publishers, p. 159.
5. Bob, Mullan (1997). *op. cit.,* p. 157.
6. Unnikrishnan, Namita and Bajpai, Shailaja (1996). *The Impact of Television Advertising on Children,* New Delhi, Sage Publications, p. 349.
7. Messenger Maire Davies (2001). *op. cit.,* quotes from the speech of John Major see; p. 156.
8. Unnikrishnan, Namita and Bajpai, Shailaja quote from National Coalition on Television Violence News Vol. 13 No. 1-4, Jan-April 1992 Campaign Illinois USA, see Unnikrishnan *et al., op. cit.,* p. 107.
9. Messenger (2001). *op. cit.,* p. 22, Quotes from Gunter and Mc Aleer (1990) *Children and Television: The One-Eyed Monster,* London Routledge.
10. Messenger Maire Davies (2001). *op. cit.,* p. 169.
11. Unnikrishnan, Namita and Bajpai, Shailaja (1996). *op. cit.,* p. 107.
12. Bob, Mullan (1997). *op. cit.,* p. 173, *Elizabeth Newson: Video Violence and Protection of Children* (1994).
13. Bob, Mullan (1997). *op. cit.,* p. 174.
14. Messenger Marie Davies (2001). Quotes from Ulla Carlsson and Celia Feilizen (1998) *Children, Media and Violence,* p. 157.

15. Messenger Maire Davies (2001). *op. cit.*, p. 163.
16. Win, Marie (1998). *The lug-in-Drug*, Penguin, Harmondsworth.
17. Messenger Maire Davies (2001). *op. cit.*, p. 140.
18. See UN Convention on the Right of the Child, see Mssenger, Maire, Davies *op. cit.*, pp. 27-28.
19. James, Oliver (2009). "Why television is bad to children's health" in the *The Hindu*, 8 June 2009.
20. Bob, Mullan (1997). *op. cit.*, p. 156.
21. Page, David and William, Crawley (2001). Quote from Anjali, Monteiro, Mumbai, in *Satellites over South Asia*, New Delhi, Sage, p. 150.
22. Messenger Maire Davies (2001). *op. cit.*, p. 164.
23. *The Hindu*, 27th July, 2007.
24. Bob, Mullan (1997). *op. cit.*, p. 178.
25. GOI (Government of India). *The Cable Act*.
26. *The Hindu*, 12th December, 2008.

10

Summary and Conclusions

Artistic and cultural activities of man date back to the pre-historic period. In a sense, man has a history because he has a culture.[1] The term culture itself was associated for a long period with the tillage of the soil, implying agriculture. Subsequently, it came to be associated with the cultivation of the mind with which artistic activities became the main focus of attention in so far as culture is concerned. With such a change, art was looked upon as a spiritual activity relying more on mental faculties rather than on material resources. Nevertheless, improvements in material conditions of life assumed a role in the growth and development of cultural and artistic activities, as material resources are required for the subsistence of the artists.

Over the years, there has been tremendous expansion and diversification of cultural and artistic activities. Technological inventions have been of crucial importance in this process of diversification of art. During the modern period, artistic activities could acquire the characteristics of an industry with varied dimensions thanks to technological advancement. The inventions of the printing press and photography have been key players in the emergence of an industry around culture which has been christened culture industry by Horkheimer and Adorno of the Frankfurt School. Socio-economic developments in the Western countries had also a say in the evolution of culture industry. In turn, culture industry became a regular economic activity engaging in the production and distribution of cultural products on commercial lines. The very fact that culture industry is engaged in the production and distribution of non-material products makes it different from other industries. Apparently, any study on the culture industry calls for new norms and yardsticks.

Television is one among those industries which have evolved around cultural activities of one kind or other. Television is an epoch-making invention which has affected all facets of life of man far beyond the imagination of his forefathers, that too within a short period of its invention. People curtail many of their other activities to find time for viewing television programmes. Television so to say, colonises leisure time. At the same time, it has grown as an economic activity by generating income and providing employment on a large scale. As an activity, television is concerned with the creation of texts and their transmission as programmes practically all the 24 hours a day both with the aid of advanced technological instruments. Notwithstanding the cultural roots of the programmes, they are produced on factory lines as commodities for sale in the market.

Though studies on television are galore, most of them deal either with its cultural, technological or communication aspects. Practically, no study seems to have been made on the economics of television. Nevertheless, as indicated in the Introduction, Horkheimer Max and Adorno T.W. of the Frankfurt school were able to sense the emergence of an industry around culture and art which they termed culture industry. They were actually appalled at the degradation of art at the behest of invested capital. However, they have not elaborated further on the concept except to draw a pessimistic picture of the whole issue. At the same time, television was in its infancy when they wrote and naturally they were not in a position to comprehend the future course of development. The present study is undertaken as practically no work on the economics of television seems to have come out, notwithstanding the growth of television as a gigantic enterprise. Ipsofacto, the attempt in the present study is to delineate the modus operandi of cultural industry with special reference to television in India as the theme.

The programmes which are transmitted through television are by themselves service products rooted in culture. They therefore fall within the ambit of Janus-faced cultural services, in which as indicted in Chapter 2, cultural contents and material ways of conveyance are equally important. Since it is a service activity, the programmes which form the output in television render any value as and when they are actually utilized by the audience. Television is a technological instrument through which communication can be made easily to a large number of people. Naturally, concepts relating to communication also become relevant to understand the working of television. Among them, play element of communication becomes more appropriate as television is invariably used for entertainment rather than creating any cathartic effect. Within the contours of the aforesaid concepts, the main issues investigated in the study are: how an industry could grow around culture, what is the product mix of television, how marketing is undertaken, what is the yardstick for valuing the output, should there be any regulation on TV and so on. Since economic norms and cultural genres coalesce in a branch of culture industry like television, a multi-dimensional and multi perspectival approach was adopted for uncovering the various issues posed in the study.

After presenting the theme, the conceptual formation of the study, the main issues and the methodology of the study in the Introduction, the study proceeds to provide a brief account of the evolution of an industry around culture. Culture, in its various manifestations bestows a sense of security and tranquility in the life of human beings. Though art and culture as such are supposed to form the superstructure, they cannot grow without the means provided by the economic 'base' created by the ordinary labour. In turn, art has widened further with the rise in productivity. Artists themselves were supported by society at large in the past. Towards the end of Seventeenth century, artists started to turn to the market to get their due share. Side by side, technology has been making progress and technology became a handmaid in the evolutionary progress of art. With the active involvement of technology in the actual evolution of art, commodification of art became another reality. Subsequently, production of art acquired the characteristics of an industry with culture industry becoming the latest form in the evolution of art. Television, has grown as a distinct category among the different categories of culture industry engaging in the production of a wide variety of cultural products and services.

Technological innovation is of paramount importance to the growth of any industry. Television is no exception to this general pattern. In fact, the history of television is driven by technological innovation of one kind or other from the very beginning. However, technological innovation by itself cannot lead to an automatic evolution of any industry. Instead, financial resource on a large scale is a vital requirement for the emergence of an industry. In the case of television, the transformation of various cultural formats as commodities forms another side in its emergence as an industry. All those aspects pertaining to the evolution of television as an industry from its beginning are delineated in Chapter 3.

Works on the development of television had its origin on parallel lines in different parts of the world from the closing decades of Nineteenth century. It culminated in the public broadcasting of TV on 2 November 1936 in London by BBC. Though the Britishers stole the march, the Americans were not far behind. They were able to demonstrate their capability by a public broadcasting of television in 1939. Activities relating to television suspended during the Second World War period, were revived with additional vitality once the War was over. Further improvements were soon to take place in the technology relating to television. The most important among them were the introduction of colour, cable networks and satellite transmission. With the entry of satellite in the field, television has been transformed itself as a transnational phenomenon.

As mentioned earlier, capital resources are needed for exploiting technological innovations for industrial purposes. The Americans were the first to sense the economic potentiality of television and accordingly organized it on business lines. In fact, it was some of the business establishments like the RCA, which initiated the experimentations for the invention of television. At the instance of the US government, the television stations were spatially distributed throughout the US in such a way as to ensure viewership to the people in all parts of the state. These stations were brought under national networks for business purposes. Thus three networks, viz; the NBC, CBS and ABC were organized in the USA during the formative days of television. These networks arrange the distribution of programmes and the sharing of receipts among the affiliates. Television became a big business in quick succession and almost all the stations were able to make huge profit from the beginning. Besides the commercial stations, large numbers of Public Service Broadcasting Stations, mainly for educational purposes were also established.

Being a branch of culture industry, TV is concerned with the production of cultural products of varying nature termed texts. They can be divided into three categories comprising those providing entertainment, instruction and information. Dramas, documentaries, soap operas, films etc. form the important entertainment programmes. Even news and informational programmes are narrated in an entertainment style. Most of the television formats and templates were developed during the early experimental years of 1960s and 1970s.

Thus there is a fusion of technology, economics and art in television. Art and economics which operate under different premises are made to coalesce through technology. The modi operandi of television are being reshaped with further changes and developments in technology like internet and digital camera etc.

How TV reached India, its evolution over the years and the significance of television as an industry form the theme of Chapter 4. Television reached India in a humble way, under a UNESCO scheme in the year 1959. Progress was very slow during the initial years. It was the Asian Games of 1982, which gave a boost to television in India. By that time, colour was also introduced in the country. Till the beginning of 1990s, TV was organized as a state monopoly. With the liberalization initiated in 1990s private channels also began to appear in India.

Indian channels like Zee, Surya and Asianet were soon to be started. Side by side, the invasion of the Indian market by foreign channels also became a fait accompli. Thus, foreign channels like STAR, Sony, MTV etc. were also in the fray. Since then, the penetration of TV was spectacular. As indicated in Chapter 4, there were only 3 million TV sets in the country in the year 1980. It went up to 27 million by 1990. However, by 1997, there were as many as 63 million sets and the number seems to have gone upto 112 million by 2005. In making such a growth, cable TV and communication satellites have played crucial roles. Cable appeared in the Indian market in a peculiar manner. The VCRs, a handy instrument suitable for meeting the entertainment needs, started to appear in the Indian sub-continent from 1980s. Sensing the growing demand for entertainment, some enterprising young men started to connect the households in their neighbourhood with cables and to exhibit films and other programs through the VCRs around 1984. This in turn could be used to exhibit TV programmes also. Since cables could exhibit programmes from different sources simultaneously, the system became very popular. By linking with satellites, cable could exhibit programmes transmitted through satellites. As a matter of fact, foreign channels appeared in the scene by taking advantage of the cable networks. Thus TV could easily penetrate in different parts of the country by availing the avenue thrown open by the cables and in turn TV became a lucrative business activity. With a capital investment of nearly Rs 40,000 crore, TV has become a major economic activity. The shares of some of the channels like Zee TV, NDTV, Surya and so on are listed even in the stock market where high prices are quoted for them. The hardware sector of television industry has also grown as a gigantic enterprise with a capital investment of Rs 8,278 crore in 2004-05. The number of colour sets produced in the country was as high as 61,41,772 in the year 2002-03.

How TV is concerned with the production of texts and their transmission as programmes is detailed in Chapter 5. Texts are creative products with signs and symbols embodied in them. Since the texts are turned out under regular factory lines, economic parameters like large scale production, standardization, differentiation enter in the picture as crucial determinants. During the formative days of television in India, the product mix was very limited in size. With as many as 261 channels transmitting programmes all the 24 hours a day, the programmes would cover more than one million hours. Apparently, a wide variety of programmes are produced every year. As seen in the Chapter 5, the situation with a wide range of programmes can be compared to a supermarket. Programmes are broadly divided into information programmes, educational programmes, and entertainment programmes. Informational programmes comprise mostly news. Conveyance of news forms one of the important functions of television. Television has become the source for news for well over 75 per cent of the population in most of the advanced countries. India is not far behind with television serving as a source of news for more than half the number of people in India. All the channels except the specialized channels like sports, music, cartoon, etc., transmit news daily in the morning, afternoon and evening. News itself falls into four categories viz. world, national, regional and local.

News forms an event which has to be gathered and processed. While doing so, exaggerated versions and personal bias are to be avoided. A later development is the presentation of what is known as tabloid news. Sensational items are exaggerated for the purpose of attracting the attention of the audience. Luckily tabloid news has not gained undue importance in India. Another branch, which has emerged is the investigating journalism. Very often the innocent relatives and bystanders are being harassed and grilled under the guise of investigating journalism. Discussion of current affairs with a panel of experts forms another format. Very often, such discussions in India lack credibility and objectivity. Educational and development programmes form another category of programmes. They constituted more than two-fifths of the programmes in our country even upto the beginning of 1990s. They were given undue importance because TV was regarded as a development fostering activity from the beginning. The importance given to such programmes has declined with the entry of private channels and the introduction of commercialism in television.

Entertainment programmes constitute the third category. They have gained importance at the expense of educational programmes. Even channels which specialize in religious or scientific themes broadcast entertainment programmes on an increasing scale during recent years. In this connection Edison's apprehension of cinema transforming as an entertainment toy has proved to be correct in the case of television also. We in India, were nurturing TV as a development fostering agent from its formative days. With the entry of private channels TV has been transformed totally as an entertainment medium. At present, even Doordarshan devotes more attention to entertainment programmes.

It is the presence of entertainment programmes which entitles television to be reckoned as a branch of culture industry. The unprecedented growth of television stems primarily because of its tilt in favour of entertainment programmes. However, it was the large scale presence of entertainment programmes which has attracted the wrath of Horkheimer and Adorno on culture industry which in their opinion is corrupt to the core.

Most of the formats which were evolved in the West during the formative days of television are adopted in India also. Thus, tele-serials, soaps, sitcoms, movies docudramas etc. evolved in the West find prominent place among the entertainment programmes in India. Among them tele-serials are perhaps the most important. In shaping the tele-serial, elements of three sources viz; radio, theatre and feature films are appropriated liberally. Among them the influence of films is more deep rooted. Many factors account for the deeper influence of films on serials. First, tele-serials represent only an improved version of cinematic technique. Second, the presence of a large number of ex-film artists in the serials makes the influence stronger. With the theatre-cum film background tele-serials are able to command high popularity in India. Almost all the channels vie with each other in telecasting serials after serials during prime time.

Much before the formation of tele-serials another format had arrived in India from foreign lands. It is the soap opera, an important genre which had its origin in the US. The thematic structure of soap operas is the presentation of never ending narratives with each episode containing an unanswered question. Many of them revolve round the tensions between mothers-in-law and daughters-in-law. Soap operas remain the most popular shows especially with women audience. As a matter of fact, tele serials are only an improved version of soap operas. The beginning was made with, Hum Log in 1984-85 followed by Bunyad, Ramayana and Mahabharat and so on. Mahabharat had as mentioned in Chapter 5, entranced 300 million viewers for an hour every Sunday for 20 months.

Film and film based programmes are another category of entertainment programmes catered by television. At least one motion picture is transmitted by each channel everyday. In short, the influence of film on TV is deep rooted. Though the emergence of television has adversely affected film industry, it could retain its hold through its direct or indirect influence on serials and other formats. Nevertheless, the manner in which entertainment is being promoted is not free from criticism. Very often entertainment programmes project sex and violence with impunity. Such a trend seems to have grown as an outcome of the influence of films.

Sports form another important category of programmes. They are perhaps the most important entertainment programmes next to tele-serials. While tele-serials and other cinematic formats fall within the ambit of culture proper, sports cannot be regarded as a cultural activity proper. Nevertheless, sports are associated with television from its formative days. As a matter of fact, there are sports which owe their popularity to television and there are television channels which owe their success and in some cases their very existence to sports.[2] Television could bring wide popularity for cricket in the country. The names of some of the cricket celebrites are even in the lips of the kids of the kindergarten. Reality shows depending on internet and digital camera is another entertainment format which has gained popularity during recent years.

TV channels which produce and transmit programmes are organized as corporate enterprises. While some of them are affiliates to multinational corporations, others combine broadcasting with other business activities. According to the Indian standards, a channel requires a capital investment of about Rs. 500 million. Recurring cost exceeds Rs. 100 million. Cost of production of a programme for 30 minutes duration can very well be about Rs. 1,50,000. Since the cost is so high, channels by themselves may not be producing all the programmes. Instead, certain concerns specializing in the production of programmes and serials have come into being. There are at present approximately 6,000 such firms operating in our country.

Channels engage in the creation or rather production of text at high cost for making a profit by selling them in the market. Since the competition is very high with a plethora of channels operating in the field, the products are standardized and massified for facing the competition in the market. In so doing, cultural quality gets diluted and economic norms come to the fore.

As indicated in Chapter 6, marketing itself is a bit complicated affair for various reasons. The very nature of output itself adds complication in the marketing of television. Texts are supposed to be the output of the television industry. However, texts as such, are of no use without getting transmitted. Apparently, transmission becomes an equally important productive activity. At the same time, the programmes have to be seen and enjoyed by the audience, if at all they are to become income generating products. In so doing, as in the case of any service activity, the actual utilization becomes the output creating and income generating activity. However, the problem is, how to measure the output as television is invariably a free service in most of the countries. An equally baffling problem is, how television earns an income by selling its services if it is a free service. Evidently, certain new norms become inevitable in the marketing of television.

In the normal sense, demand becomes effective only with the actual purchase of the commodity. Since the audience does not pay practically anything for viewing the programmes, somebody else might be paying the bill. This is rendered possible by resorting to what is termed dual product marketing by which channels also sell their airtime to businessmen in addition to the sale of regular programmes to the audience. Business people who purchase airtime make use of it as an effective means for advertising their products in the market. Thus the advertiser appears in the picture in a big way as the defacto purchaser in the marketing of TV. However, the volume of advertisement depends on the size of audience who watches the programmes in a particular channel. Apparently, an equilibrating process with the demand represented by the advertiser and the supply represented by the audience who becomes the consumer-cum producer of the output is inherent in the marketing of TV.

In television, a branch of culture industry artistic labour provides an important input in the production or rather creation of texts, the main product of the industry. However, the standard variables like labour-supply, wage determination, conditions of service etc., are unsuitable to explain the labour market behaviour in television industry, as artists form a class of, 'free' labour as opposed to the ordinary labour and the texts are products of art. Apparently new yardsticks, very often indirect in nature become inevitable, to understand the modus operandi of artistic labour market. Accordingly, certain level of autonomy is conferred on them and remuneration is paid on the basis of contract. However, widespread inequality prevails in so far as the payment of remuneration to different classes of artists is concerned. Some of the serial actors render their service at very low rate in anticipation of a bright future.

Programmes are telecast for the audience to view the them. It is believed that television is able to make far reaching changes in the social, cultural, economic and political life of man. As an author succinctly puts, television has touched the audience at the most superficial levels without seeming to accept responsibility for its own consequences.[3] How the audience view TV and the impact thereof on various facets of life based on the findings of a field study, form the theme in the next Chapter. It also contains an account of the profile of the audience, their viewing habits, their preference to different kinds of programmes.

With the development of the satellite technology, progrmme from any part of the world can penetrate in other parts easily. National frontiers have become irrelevant in controlling TV programmes from outside the country. Proliferation of channels has become a reality and with each channel carrying signals from far and wide, it has become difficult to control even the programmes originating within the country itself. At the same time, most of the governments have adopted a laissez-faire policy in so far as television is concerned. However, as mentioned earlier, TV is a powerful medium capable of making far reaching changes in the life of man. If so the question is, should the state leave everything to the free play of the market? Does not the state have a moral obligation to safeguard the well-being of the citizens by regulating and even interfering in an enterprise like television?

As indicated earlier, most of the programmes are mere commercial products designed to attract large number of audience. Very often the language, the presentation and the theme are suitably modified in such a way as to meet the commercial requirements. Invariably, vulgar themes with obscene language get undue importance in the programme. As stated earlier, sex and violence find a prominent place in many programmes. Needless to say, programmes of such a nature are potent with undesirable consequences. As a mater of fact, TV has been accused as the instigator of the incidences of violence, sexual assault, divorce etc. which are discernable during recent year on an increasing scale. Such evil consequences call for the interference in the affairs of television.

A far more serious aspect of the issue relates to the impact of television on children. With the widespread penetration of TV, children are invariably found in front of the TV set everyday. In many instances, TV has become some sort of a baby sitter. When TV is such an inseparable companion, it would certainly be playing a key role in moulding the behavioural pattern and character formation of the children. It is all the more serious because children who are immature class can be easily influenced. Moreover, the habits formed during childhood cannot easily be rectified. At the same time, TV programmes contain a relentless diet of violence and other kinds of filth from which the children must be protected.

However, the problem is, how to protect the children and also the society at large from the evil influence of TV. One of the policies suggested and adopted is to regulate the timing of the programmes as is pursued in countries like Great Britain under what is known as family viewing policy. Children can easily evade this policy as they can see any programme when parents are absent. Another measure is to impose a code on the exhibition of programmes. However, the channels may not follow the code strictly.

Imposition of censorship forms another step which can be adopted in the matter. It was a measure adopted from ancient past. Imposition of censorship has been criticized as its indiscriminate use can be a threat to artistic freedom of expression. On the other hand, most of the programmes are pure commercial commodities with very little artistic content. When censorship is imposed, it is not art that is being restricted but commercial practices. However, the problem is, how to impose censorship effectively when large number of channels, some of them from foreign lands continuously transmit programmes. The proposed Content Code making regulations more explicit, though opposed by the channels, appears to be a step in the right direction. Even then, careful monitoring and watchful attention are required, if at all the programmes are to be regulated and controlled.

In sum, television industry, a progeny of technology has only a history of about sixty years with its real beginnings after the Second World War. Within this short period, it has as Shanahan and Morgan enjoin, permeated every corner of public and private space, shaping consciousness, defining our reality, drawing us together and pulling us apart in ways that will uniquely, enshrine this historical period as the age of television.[4]

However, the position of television as the premiere culture industry is being challenged by the same technology which has fostered it from its very inception. Among them the challenge from technological innovations like the internet is far more serious than from any other side. It is somewhat similar to the threat to film industry when television emerged in the scene. Television also will have to readjust and modify its modus operandi in the years to come as the film industry did a few years earlier. In fact, new strategies seem to be in the offing in the West from what Meyer says in the matter, is taken as an indicator. He says "TV is evolving towards a new paradigm whereby television consumption will be less linear and more interactive, personal and nomadic."[5] The growing popularity of reality TV fostered by the internet and digital technology points to such a possibility in India also.

NOTES AND REFERENCES

1. Godelier, Maurice (1986). *The Material and the Manual: Thought, Economy and Society* (Translated by Martin Thom; Norfolk, Verso) p. 1.
2. Barnet Steven (1998). "Sport" in Smith Anthony (ed); *Television: An International history,* Oxford University Press, p. 85.
3. Smith, Anthony (1998) "Introduction" in Smith Anthony (ed). *op. cit.,* p. 5.
4. Shanahan, James and Morgan, Michael (1999). *Television and Its Viewers: Cultivation Theory and Research,* Cambridge University Press p. 2.
5. Meyer, Lawrence (2006). "Communication and Strategies" in MPRA Paper No. 3517 posted in June 2006.

Bibliography

Adorno, T.W. and Max, Horkheimer (1972). "The Culture Industry: Enlightenment as Mass Deception" in James Curran (ed.) *Mass Communication and Society*, London, Open University.

Agarwal, Binod C. (1986). *Communication Research for Development: The ISRO Experience*, Delhi, Concept.

Alberran, Alan (2003). *Media Economies: Understanding Markets, Industries and Concepts*, Oxford, Blackwell Publishing Company.

Altschull, Herbert J. (1995). *Agents of Power: The Media and Public Policy*, New York, Longman Publishers.

Andrejevic, Mark (2004). *Reality TV; The Work of Being Watched*, Lanham Rowman & Littlefield Publishers Inc.

Bertold, Brecht (1990). *Poems and Songs from Plays*, London, Mac Millan.

Bhat, S.C. (1994). *Satellite Invasion of India*, New Delhi, Gyan Publishers.

Bignell, Jonathan (1980). *An Introduction to Television Studies*, London, Routledge.

Bitner, John R. (1980). *Broadcasting and Television: An Introduction*, New Jersey, Prentice Hall.

Blumber Jay, G. "The New Television Market Place; Imperatives and Implication" in James Curran and Michael Gurevitch (ed.) *Mass Media and Society*, London, Edward Arnold, a Division of Hodder and Stongton.

Bob, Mullan (1997). *Consuming Television*, Oxford, Blackwell Publishers.

Burger, Anna (1970). *Economic Problems of Consumer Services*, Budapest, Akademia Kiado.

Business India, May 6, 2007.

Butcher, Melissa (2003). *Transnational Television: Culture Identity and Change*, New Delhi, Sage Publications.

Chris, Barker (1997). *Global Television*, Oxford, Blackwell Publishers.

Collingwood, R.G. (1938). *The Principles of Art*, Clarendon, Oxford University Press.

David, Page and William, Crawley (2001). *Satellite Over South Asia: Broadcasting Culture and Public Interest*, New Delhi Sage.

Davis, Maire Messenger (2001). *Dear BBC; Children, Television, Story Telling and Public Sphere*, Cambridge University Press.

Edman, Irwin (1939). *Art and the Man: A Short Introduction to Aesthetics*, New York, W.W. Norton and Company.

Edward, Buscombe (1984). "Television and Film Industry" in *Quarterly Review of Film Studies*, Vol. 9, No. 3.

Eisenstein, Elizabeth L. (1970). *Printing Press as the Agent of Change*, Cambridge, University Press.

Ernst, Fischer (1959). *The Necessity of Art: A Marxist Approach*, Penguin Books.

FICCI (2007). *The Indian Entertainment and Media Industry: A Growth Story Unfolds.*

Francoise, Benhamou (2003). "Artists' Labour Markets" in Towse Ruth (ed.) *A Handbook of Cultural Economics*, Cheltenham, Edgar Elgar.

Godelier, Maurice (1986). *The Mental and The Material: Thought, Economy and Society*, Translated by Martin Thom; Norfolk, Verso.

GOI (Government of India) (1960). *India 1960*, New Delhi, Ministry of Information and Broadcasting.

—— (1964). *India 1964*, New Delhi, Ministry of Information and Broadcasting.

—— (1971-72). *Annual Survey of Industries 1971-72*, New Delhi, Central Statistical Organisation.

—— (1978). *Report of the Working Group on the Autonomy of Akashwani and Doordarshan* Vol. II, New Delhi, Ministry of Information and Broadcasting.

—— (1995). *Doordarshan* 1995, Audience Research Unit; Directorate General Doordarshan, New Delhi.

—— (2002). *Doordarshan India 2002*, New Delhi, Ministry of Information and Broadcasting.

—— (2002-03). *Annual Survey of Industries 2002-03*, New Delhi, Central Statistical Organisation.

—— (2005-06). *Annual Report*, New Delhi, Ministry of Information and Broadcasting.

—— (2005-06). *Annual Survey of Industries 2005-06*, New Delhi, Central Statistical Organisation.

—— (2005-06). *Prasar Bharatti: Information, Education and Entertainment: Annual Report* (Broadcasting Corporation of India.

Golding, Peter (1984). *The Mass Media*, London, Longman.

Gordan, George N. (1975). *Communications and Media: Constructing a Cross Discipline*, New York, Communication Art Books.

Gouldner, Alan (1990). "Ideology, Cultural Apparatus and New Consciousness Industry" in Jeffrey, Alexander (ed.) *Culture and Society*, Cambridge University Press.

Harless, James (1990). *Mass Communication: An Introductory Survey*, Dubuque, Wn. C. Publishers.

Heilburn James and Charles Gray M. (2001). *The Economies of Art and Culture*, Cambridge University Press.

Hesmondhalgh, David (2001). *The Culture Industries*, New Delhi, Sage Publications.

Hugh Fordian (1975). *The World of Entertainment*, New York, Doubleday.

Jacquetta, Hawkes and Leonard, Woolley (1963). *History of Mankind; Culture and Scientific Development*, Vol. I, *Pre-History and Beginnings of Civilisation*, London, George Allen and Unwin.

James, Curran (ed.) (1977). *Mass Communication and Society*, London, Open University Setbook.

James, Shanahan and Michael, Morgan (1999). *Television and Its Viewers; Cultivation Theory and Research*, Cambridge, University Press.

Jeevan Telecasting Corporation Ltd. *Annual Report 2005-06* (Kochi).

Johnson Kirk (2000). *Television and Social Change in India*, New Delhi, Sage Publications.

Joseph, K.V. (1990). "Economics of Art" in P.R. Gopinathan Nair, *Economy, Planning and Policies*, Delhi, Concept Publication.

Joseph, K.V. (1990). "The Impact of New Media on Film Industry" in *Loyola Journal of Social Sciences*, Vol. IV, No. 1, 1990.

Joseph, K.V. (1997). "Policy Options in Film Industry in India", paper presented during the 28th Film Festival of India held in Trivandrum, Jan. 1997.

Joyce, Carey (1958). *Art and Reality*, Cambridge University Press.

Kenneth, Boulding (1973). "Towards the Development of a Cultural Economics" in Louis Sneider (ed.) (1973), *Idea of Culture in Social Sciences*, Cambridge University Press.

Keval, Kumar J. (1989). *Mass Communication in India*, Bombay, Jaico Publications.

Kohli, Anitha (2003). *The Indian Media Business*, New Delhi, Sage Publications.

Kunhikrishnan, K. (2006). "Television-Obstacles behind the Scene" (Mal.) in *Mathrubhoomi Daily* (7.9.2006).

Lembo, Ron (2000). *Thinking Through Television*, Cambridge, University Press.

Lodziak, Conrad (1986). *The Power of Television: A Critical Appraisal*, London, France, Pinter.

Mahajan, Kamalesh (1990). *Television and Women Development*, New Delhi, Classical Publishing Company.

Manle, Christopher (2003). 'Television' in Towse Ruth (ed.) *A Handbook of Cultural Economics*, Cheltenham, Edward Elgar.

Martin, Barbero Jesus (1993). *Communication, Culture and Hegemony*, London, Sage Publications.

Marwin, Harris (1979). *Cultural Maternalism*, New Folk, Random Press.

Marx, Karl (1958). *Marx, Engels on Literature and Art*, Moscow, Progressive Publications.

Mc Phail, Thomas, L. (2006). *Global Communication Theories: Stakeholders and Trends*, Oxford, Blackwell Publishers.

Mc Quail, Dennis (1987). *Mass Communication Theory*, London, Sage.

Meir, Blake and Andrew, Nava (ed.) (1997). *Buy this Book; Advertisement and Consumption*, London, Routledge Taylor Frances Group.

Melkote, Srinivas R. (1991). *Communication and Development in Third World Countries*, New Delhi, Sage Publications.

Melvin, L De Fleur and Sandra Ball-Rokeach (1982). *Theories of Mass Communication*, NewYork Longman.

Michael, Gurevitch, Tony Bennet, James Curran and Janer Woodlacott (eds.) (1982). *Culture Society and Media*, London, Methuen.

Mitra, Anand (1993). *Television in India: A Study of Mahabharat*, Delhi, Sage Publication.

Negrine, Ralph and Pathana-ssopoulos Stylianos (1990). *The Internationalisation of Television*, London, Pinther Publishers.

Newson, Elizabeth (1994). *Video Violence and Protection of Children* (Mimeo).

Oliver, Boyd-Barret and Peter, Braham (1987). *Media, Knowledge and Power*. London, Crom Helm in Association with Open University.

Oommen, M.A. and Joseph, K.V. (1981). *Economics of Film Industry in India*, Gurgaon, Academic Press.

— — (1991). *Economics of Indian Cinema*, Delhi, Oxford and I.B.H.

Osborne, Harold (1968). *Aesthetics and Art Theory: An Historical Introduction*, London, Longman Green & Co.

Otte Claus (1984). *Contradiction of Welfare State* (London, Huchison).

Patterson, Richard (1998). "Non-fiction Television" in Smith Antony (ed.) *Television an International History*, New York, Oxford University Press.

Paul, Hartman; Patel, B.R. and Anitha, Dighe (1989): *The Mass Media and Village Life*, New Delhi, Sage Publications.

Pick, John (1986). *Managing the Art: The British Experience*, London, Rhinegold Publishing Company.

Price, Monroe E. and Stefaan, G. Verliulist (ed.) (1998). *Broadcasting Reforms in India: Media Law in Global Perspective*, Delhi Oxford University Press.

Raj Gopalan, V. (2000). *Television Journalism (Mal.)* Kottayam, Current Books.

Rao, B.S.S. (1992). *Television and Rural Development* (Delhi, Concept).

Reddy, Usha Vyasalu (1996). "RipVan Winkle: A Story of Indian Television" in David French and Michael Richard *Contemporary Television: Easterm Perspective, op. cit.*

Rosen, Sherwin (1986). "The Theory of Equalising Differences" in O. Ashenfelter and R. Layard (ed.), *Handbook of Labour Economics, Vol. 1,* Amsterdam, North Holland.

Sardesai, Rajdeep (2006). "Pushing the Boundaries" in *Seminar,* May 2006.

Saundra, Hydels and Daria, Ulloth (1978). *Broadcasting: Introduction to Radio and Television,* New York, D. Van Nostral Company.

Schramm, Wilbur and William, Porter (1982): *Men, Women, Messages and Media: Managing Media Organisation,* New York, Harper Row Publishers.

Shanahan, James and Morgan, Michael (1999). *Television andIts Viewers Cultivation Theory and Research,* Cambridge, University Press.

Shankleman—Lucy King (2000): *Managing Media Organisation,* London, Routledge, Taylor Frances.

Sherwin, Rosen (1981). "The Economics of Superstars" in *American Economic Review, Vol. 71,* Dec. 1981.

Sinha, Aravind (1996). "Development Dilemmas of Indian Television" in David French *et al. Contemporary Television: Eastern Perspective,* New Delhi, Sage.

—— (1989). *India's Information Revolution,* New Delhi, Sage.

——and Roger, Everett M. (2000). *India's Communication Revolution,* New Delhi, Sage Publications.

Smith, Anthony (ed.) (1998). *Television: An International History,* Oxford University Press.

Steinert, Heinz (2003). *Culture Industry,* Translated by Sally Ann Spencer, Cambridge, Polity Press.

Stempel, III, Guido, H. and Westley, H. Bruce (1989): *Research Methods in Mass Communicatioin,* New Jersey, Prentice Hall.

Stephenson, W. (1975). *The Play Theory of Communication,* University of Chicago Press.

Thapar, Kiran (2006). 'A Critique of Television News' in *Seminar,* May 2006.

The Economist, 6 January 2007 "The Future of BBC".

The Hindu, 20 June 2007.

The Hindu, 24 March 2007.

Thomas, Amos Owen (2005). *Imagi -Nations and Borderless Television,* New Delhi, Sage.

Throsby, David (1994). 'Production and Consumption of Art: A View of Cultural Economics' in *Journal of Cultural Economics*, Vol. XXXII, March 1994.

— — (2001). *Economics and Culture* (Cambridge, University Press).

Tiziana, Cuceia (2003). "Contingent Valuation" in Towse Ruth (ed.) *A Handbook of Cultural Economics*, Cheltenham, Edward Elgar Publishing Company.

Tolstoi Leo (1975). *Essays on Art*, Oxford, University Press.

Towse, Ruth (2003). *A Handbook of Cultural Economics*, Cheltenham Edward Elgar.

Tracey, Michael (1998). "Drama and Entertainment" in Smith Antony (ed.) *op. cit.*

Trivedi, Harshad R. (1991). *Mass Media and New Horizons: Impact of TV and Video in Urban Milieu*, Delhi, Concept.

UNESCO Statistical Year Books 1994 and 1999.

Unnikrishnan, Namita and Shailaja, Bajpai (1996). *The Impact of Television Advertisement on Children*, New Delhi, Sage Publication.

Vaquez, Adolf Sanchez (1973). *Art and Society: Essays in Marxist Aesthetics*, London, Merlin Press.

Vogel, Harold L. (2001). *Entertainment and Industry Economics*, Cambridge University Press.

Walter, Benjamin (1997). "Work of Art in the age of Mechanical Reproduction" in J. Curran (ed.) *Mass Communication and Society*, *op. cit.*

Ward, Ken (1989). *Mass Communication and Modern World*, London, Macmillan Education.

Williams, Raymond (1975). *Television; Technology and Cultural Form*, London, Routledge.

— — (1993). "Advertising the Magic System" in Simon During (ed.) *Cultural Studies*, London, Routledge.

Wilson, Roy, and Stein, L.E. (1989). *Mass Media and Mass Culture*, New York, Random House.

Withers, Glenn (2003). "Broadcasting" in Ruth Towse (ed.) *A Handbook of Cultural Economics*, Cheltenham, Edward Elgar.

Index